Unleashed is a biblically bala  udy of the doctrine of sanctification liever seeking to grow in being co will be blessed and helped by this wo...

Daniel L. Akin, President, Southeastern Baptist
Theological Seminary

Dr. Eric Mason has constructed a theological treatise on sanctification that transfers from the kitchen table to the seminary classroom. His transparency, authenticity, and theological accuracy join forces to help us see ourselves within God's transformative work. *Unleashed* is to be read and discussed by believers and by those seeking to discover and follow the Way.

Stephen G. Brown, Pastor/Servant Leader

Praise God for a book on growing in Christ that is rooted deeply in the holiness of God yet is immensely practical on what that means for everyday life.

Matt Chandler, Lead Pastor of The Village Church,
President of Acts 29

Unleashed reminds us that throughout the process of spiritual growth, it is Christ who initiates, sustains, fulfills, and perfects our life in Him. A very practical read.

K. A. Ellis, President and Co-Founder of
Ellis Perspectives and the Makazi Institute

Having been a part of watching the journey of Eric and his family for the last few decades it is clear to me that God's hand is on him. Just looking at the table of contents in this book reminds me of some of the chapters of his life and how God has grown him tremendously. This book flows from God willing and working His good pleasure in Eric, and we are being invited to do the same. God is at work in all His people, and it is our job to submit to and connect to what He uses to grow us! Read *Unleashed* and be unleashed to maximize the growth that God has in store for you!

Tony Evans, Senior Pastor of Oak Cliff Bible Fellowship, President of The Urban Alternative

Dr. Eric Mason does it again with a heartfelt, biblically sound, and inspirational book on God's goal in our redemption (Rom. 8:29), our spiritual formation. *Unleashed* is a book that all should use as a personal reminder of time with Christ and being transformed by Christ, it also provides tools to equip your teams and church members if you're in pastoral ministry. He addresses sanctification in a clear and concise manner that will leave you encouraged and compelled to intentionally embrace your personal transformation with joy and vigor.

Jerome Gay Jr., Vision Church

I love this new book by Eric Mason. If you are like me and spent too much time in your spiritual journey trying to do something for God before discovering the difference in something done by God, this volume is for you. As I read it, I found myself humming a great old hymn I memorized decades ago—"Grace that exceeds our sin and our guilt . . . grace that is greater than all our sin!" Read this and reap!

O. S. Hawkins, President/CEO, GuideStone Financial Resources

If you are seriously interested in moving your walk in life to a deeper level, then this work by Pastor Eric Mason, *Unleashed,* will be the book you want to read. In *Unleashed: Being Conformed to the Image of Christ,* Pastor Mason delves into the topic of sanctification. Using the Word of God, he provides you with the tools necessary to unleash the power that comes only through a closer walk with Christ.

John K. Jenkins Sr., Senior Pastor
First Baptist Church of Glenarden

My pastor, Dr. Eric Mason, has challenged the church to step out of passivity and aggressively pursue God's means of spiritual growth! This book is a valuable resource because it helps us look to Christ as the primary and central source of our spiritual development while motivating believers to run hard after spiritual maturity. Pastor Mason, with theological precision, has revealed to us a clear path of sanctification often overlooked in mainstream Christian thought. A must have, a must read, a must teach.

Pastor Doug Logan Jr., Founding and Lead Pastor,
Epiphany Fellowship Church, Camden, New Jersey

This book is a compelling, foundational resource on the Christian life. It outlines the God-sanctioned process to make us Christlike. Growth is not the product of what we like or trafficking in the spiritual "experiences" we enjoy; it is faithfully honoring and applying the eternally transforming resources my dear friend Eric Mason points to in this important book. Thank you, Eric, for showing us how we can draw near to our Savior, the lover of our souls.

Crawford W. Loritts Jr., Author, Speaker,
Radio Host, Senior Pastor of Fellowship Bible Church,
Roswell, Georgia

Unleashed will set you free from what holds you and take you more deeply into the transforming power of Jesus Christ. Eric Mason writes in compelling ways about sanctification because he has studied it carefully and lived it personally. Read and be changed forever.

James MacDonald, Senior Pastor, Harvest Bible Chapel,
Author of *Vertical Church*

This is a rich, practical book, by a wise, gifted pastor. Sanctification is not just behaving morally more often. Sanctification is an act of spirit surgery on our minds and affections, patterning us after our Lord Jesus. This book will help you know how to keep in step with the Spirit.

Russell Moore, President, Ethics & Religious
Liberty Commission, Southern Baptist Convention

Pastor Eric Mason makes the weighty topic of sanctification user-friendly for every Christian. His keen insights from the Word are given vivid clarity with his engaging illustrations and personal experience. This book doesn't just explain sanctification, it makes the reader want to pursue it in every area of life with grace, faith, and joy.

John H. Sather, National Director, Cru Inner City

Eric unpacks progressive sanctification with clear biblical exposition, theological explanation, vivid illustration, and rubber meets the road application. Anyone who wants to grow in their Christlikeness needs to read *Unleashed*.

Ikki Soma, Servant Pastor, City of Refuge Church

Unleashed: Being Conformed to the Image of Christ, is a peek behind the curtain of how God produces followers of Jesus, who resemble the one they are following.

Albert Tate, Founder and Lead Pastor, Fellowship Monrovia

In *Unleashed*, Pastor Eric Mason unpacks great news for the believer—"we get to live for Christ through the power of Christ." So often the temptation is to think that the Lord is mighty to save, but that our own might is required to grow. Ultimately, this leads to discouragement, since our own strength is limited. *Unleashed* makes clear that in every phase of life, God is at work, overseeing and superintending our lives with the goal to make us more and more like Christ. In addition to biblical examples, Pastor Mason uses powerful examples from his own life and ministry, including personal suffering, to effectively drive home this point. And yet, we are also challenged and encouraged to pursue our part of sanctification, such as studying the Word, drawing near to God in prayer, and growing through repentance. This is an important book, one that will instruct, comfort, motivate, and even excite believers as they better understand what it means to unleash the power of God in their lives.

Kim Cash Tate, Author and Bible teacher

Eric Mason's book, *Unleashed*, is a biblical and practical guide to gospel-centered sanctification. While many spiritual growth books focus on the individual and internal aspects of sanctification, this book also emphasizes the many means God has given His people for sanctification as well as land mines to avoid in the process of becoming formed into the image of Christ. Eric Mason is a man who has lived out this content as a Christian and in his role as a pastor. What he has written here is a blessing to the church.

Harvey Turner, Lead Pastor of Living Stones Church,
Regional Director of Acts 29 West

BEING CONFORMED TO THE
IMAGE OF CHRIST

UNLEASHED

ERIC MASON

B&H
PUBLISHING GROUP
NASHVILLE, TENNESSEE

Copyright © 2015 by Eric Mason
All rights reserved.
Printed in the United States of America

978-1-4336-8747-1

Published by B&H Publishing Group,
Nashville, Tennessee

Dewey Decimal Classification: 248.84
Subject Heading: CHRISTIAN LIFE \ DISCIPLESHIP \
SPIRITUAL LIFE

Unless otherwise noted all Scripture is taken from the English
Standard Version, (esv) copyright © 2001 by Crossway Bibles, a
publishing ministry of Good News Publishers. esv Text Edition:
2007. All rights reserved.

Also used: New Living Translation (nlt), copyright © 1996. Used
by permission of Tyndale House Publishers, Inc., Wheaton, IL
60189 USA. All rights reserved.

Also used: New American Standard Bible (nasb), the Lockman
Foundation, 1960, 1962, 1963, 1968, 1971, 1972, 1973, 1975, 1977,
used by permission.

Also used: New Revised Standard Version Bible (nrsv), copy-
right © 1989 the Division of Christian Education of the National
Council of the Churches of Christ in the United States of America.
Used by permission. All rights reserved.

Also used: King James Version (kjv) which is public domain.

1 2 3 4 5 6 7 8 • 19 18 17 16 15

I dedicate this book to my pastor and his wife and my church, Drs. Tony and Lois Evans and the Oak Cliff Bible Fellowship church family, who contributed the most on a practical learning level in the journey of my wife and I throughout this book. Between the years of 1995–2000 and 2002–2004, we grew deeply in this ministry as God used it as a tool in our maturity that is still bearing fruit. Thank you! ✗

CONTENTS

ACKNOWLEDGMENTS

Thanks to the whole B&H and LifeWay staff, particularly Devin Maddox and Kim Stanford for working through this document. Andrew Wolgemuth, you and your team have been very helpful in helping me work through the particulars of getting this done.

Thanks also to Dr. D. A. Carson and Dr. John Piper for giving me some thoughts on writing a work like this. Jeremiah, thank you for assisting me in getting stuff done.

Epiphany Fellowship Church body, the pastors, and staff, thank you for allowing me the bandwidth to write and put out material that will hopefully lead people to Jesus and edify the larger body of Christ in Jesus. ✗

Preface

I n city neighborhoods, you can find people hanging out outside. Especially in the spring, summer, and early fall. People will hang until the wee hours of the night talking, laughing, arguing, people-watching, or being up to no good. Hearing the stories of men and women who hang out there, you will find that some of the most gifted people have had major opportunities that have passed them by. You can find everything from people who had academic or athletic scholarships, to former business owners and artists, who have all found themselves up and then down. In a word, you find people with *potential*.

Upon hearing these extraordinary people reminisce about their past, you become baffled—baffled that individuals with so much ahead of them, so much opportunity, now find themselves in a place of stagnancy. All the opportunities that they had, were either lost by mistake, or by some tragedy. All they have to rejoice over is in the past. Those past moments become the only bright spot in their lives to the point where they haven't moved on to greater experiences and opportunities or harnessed those times to be catapulted into greater fruitfulness in life.

I would say that many Christians find themselves in these same dire straits. Many Christians love to reminisce about the glory days of their faith. They treat the Christian life like a silver, golden, and platinum age of their walk with Jesus, treating the journey with God as high moments, versus living a life of faithfulness in the faith. Hebrews 10:38 states, "but my righteous one shall live by faith." God expects our life with Him to be a marathon faith trajectory. That is, consistently enduring a journey that is empowered by faith in God.

Specifically speaking of unleashing the transformation offered to those who follow Christ by faith—of both justification and sanctification—we must not see our journey with Jesus beginning and ending with a past moment, but as a continuous journey began by God in the gospel, sustained by God in the gospel, and completed by God in the gospel. God both begins and ends our journey (Phil. 1:6). We don't do any of the above, but we must be responsible with the journey that God has begun. God superintends our journey with Him, and has expectations of us under His superintending hand (Titus 2:11–15).

As we journey into talking about spiritual growth throughout this book, it will be a refrain, sung out over and over again, that God's goal for us is to be conformed to the image of Jesus Christ (Rom. 8:29). All of the Christian life is movement toward being like the Son, toward God's likeness. All that has a beginning also bears continuation, and a finalization. My goal is to call believers to a life-style of faith by which we submit and maximize every means that God makes available to us as *He* grows and sanctifies us by faith.

Before writing this book I did not realize how many resources have been written over the years on the subject of *being conformed into the image of Christ* (sanctification). But they all have one thing in common; so many of them are all over the map in relation to *how* sanctification happens, and its role in our lives every day.

There tend to be two opposite poles of a spectrum when it comes to addressing this topic. I find that on the theological side, there are those who weigh heavy in talking about holiness being rooted in the character of God, but never really speak of how it impacts us daily until the return of Jesus. On the other side, you find pragmatic works that seek to talk about how we should work to grow ourselves but not really rooting it in what God has done for us in the Lord Jesus Christ theologically.

In essence, this is a book on *sanctification*. My goal isn't simply to drop heavy words on you; it is to root the concept of sanctification where the Bible does, in Jesus' death and resurrection by faith and continued faith (Col. 1:23). It will also be to make sure that we connect to some of the ways in which God calls us to pursue holiness (Heb. 12:14). The distinction is that our pursuit of holiness doesn't make us holy, but God does, and not pursuing holiness will end up leaving us lacking in practical holiness.

Maybe you are like one of those people I have met on my block. Maybe you *are* one of those people. The truth is, your potential is far greater than anything a scholarship, business venture, or artistic achievement could ever give you. God is ready to *unleash* the power of His Son in your life. Are you ready?

Introduction

As a pastor, I cannot tell you how many times I have heard people say, "I don't feel like I'm growing." Many Christians wrestle with this issue. I sometimes do as well.

You preachers will know what I mean. Writing a book on sanctification has been like preaching on a particular subject and God gives you a pop quiz on whether or not your life reflects what you proclaimed. As I have prepared to write, my commitment to submitting to God's sanctifying work in my life has been greatly challenged. I both feel the challenge to walk with Jesus, and I am encouraged by the hope of the gospel. Sanctification is the victorious struggle. Victorious in that Jesus has secured our sanctification, but a struggle in that we are called to be active pursuers of holiness.

Unleashed: Being Transformed into the Image of Christ is a resource for all who want to intentionally participate in their spiritual growth. First Thessalonians 4:3a says, "For this is the will of God, your sanctification." Paul also instructs, "For those whom he foreknew he also predestined to be conformed to the image of his Son, in order that he might be the firstborn among many brothers" (Rom. 8:29). God's will is not just that we be born again, but that we grow into spiritual adults. Rather, speaking the truth in love, we are to grow up in every way into Him who is the head, into Christ. Growing up as a believer is the mandate on the life of every Christian. In light of this rich reality, the believer must be clear on how we can intentionally plug into the ways in which God grows us. Everyone has wondered, *Why am I not growing?* and *Why do I feel like my life is at a standstill?* God's work in us is always in motion, but the question is: Are we submissive to His process of the work that He has in progress (2 Cor. 4:16)?

Progressive sanctification is God's dynamic process by which *He* ushers the redeemed from spiritual infancy to spiritual maturity. We do not cause our own growth, but as we pursue the holiness of Christ, the Spirit grows us as we access the means God makes available for us to grow. Therefore, God is sanctifying us, but the issue is submission to His sanctifying work. Philippians 2:12–13 drives home the point. God has already accomplished our salvation so much so that He wills us to grow and it gives Him great pleasure. The pleasure is to be like Jesus. In our sanctification we have been fully revitalized, but it is not yet fully realized!

My desire isn't to write an exhaustive book on this subject—as if I could or anyone else for that matter—but to develop a biblically based, framework-developing, practical tool to aid believers in being unleashed in and through God's means for their spiritual growth in Jesus Christ. My goal is to serve the body—the church— with a tool that helps us understand our spiritual growth and to maximize the means that God uses to conform us to the image of Jesus Christ. From a practical standpoint, my desire would be to talk about different sectors and seasons of life that are used by God to grow us.

In the Bible, it is clear that those who have repented and believed in the Good News about Jesus Christ *have been sanctified* (Rom. 8:30), *are being sanctified* (Gal. 3), and *will be sanctified* (Rom. 8:30). All of this is done in accordance with these verses, by faith in the gospel, and by activation of the Holy Spirit. He is the overseer of the whole of our sanctification (1 Thess. 4:7–8; 5:23). Moreover, the sentences in this paragraph will be the foundation of every section within this work. Without our sanctification being positioned as a total work of God, we set people up to believe that holiness depends on us and not the work of the Lord in the Spirit.

In my estimation, this subject matter is the most important for the believer. It is important because God's sanctifying work in us extends to every aspect of our lives. *Every* aspect of our lives means Christological conformity, to *everything*. That is why Paul can say "all things work together for our good" (Rom. 8:28) in the context of God's predestined work of conforming us to the divine image.

Jesus is the goal of the Christian life. Every sector of our life is a harvest field for the work of God to make us holy in Jesus. Just as a gardener uses rakes, shovels, plows, fertilizer, and pruning devices, so is every aspect of this world a means of grace for God to make us look practically like the Lord Jesus Christ. They are tools for conforming to His image. This is why Jesus in John 15:1 calls God the Father "the gardener" (NLT). The Father as Gardener is the visionary leader of our sanctification. Jesus calls Himself the *vine,* the source for how we grow. Later the Spirit is the leader to *harvest* our sanctification (John 14–17). The Spirit guides us into the means of conformity, and makes sure that the life of Jesus Christ and the direction of the Father is connected and applied to our lives. Therefore, the triune God works in concert together for our growth.

However, it is equally important to see ourselves as *active* participants in desiring God. We must take pains to embrace the means of sanctification that the Spirit leads us into. This is all done by faith in the triune God, the one God who sanctifies.

It is impossible to speak of *all* of the ways in which God sanctifies us. I want to speak of some of the *key* means of grace that God calls for our participation in as He renews us day by day (2 Cor. 4:16).

Chapter 1, called "Gospel Growth," is what I would like to call the anchor chapter. As I received great counsel in writing, one of the pitfalls could be to make people think that if they do all the things in this book they will grow themselves. Therefore, my task in this chapter is to hammer away at the fact that God, through faith in the gospel, grows us. My prayer is that the gospel will encourage, as well as convict, us to walk in empowerment to live in the image into which He is changing us.

A huge part of this will be developing a working definition from the Scriptures and church history of sanctification, and land it on the streets of our lives. Also, we must do the same with a related doctrine, namely *justification*. The purpose of this is to both distinguish and connect the two. Although both are distinct, you cannot have one without the other. I will not seek to parse how it intricately works, but I would like to talk about how they are connected without dealing with which one was first or was it a simultaneous work. There are arguments for both, yet my desire will be to look at passages that link God declaring us righteous, setting us aside in righteousness, and calling us to pursue righteousness all obtained through the precious work of Jesus Christ.

Chapter 2, "The Holy Spirit's Role in Our Growth," will also be integral to the arguments laid out in the rest of the book. God the Father wills our growth (Phil. 2:12) and is the Gardener of our growth (John 15:1); the Holy Spirit is the one who connects the means of growth we apply to the vine (Jesus) so that we may bear fruit in our season (Ps. 1:3). Although the Godhead simultaneously exists, the Holy Spirit's role is to be the increaser of our growth in holiness. Jesus spent a considerable amount of the time prior to His movement toward the cross explaining the role that the Spirit would have after the ascension. Therefore, it is impossible to become a part of the body of Jesus without the Spirit, and it is impossible to grow as a believer without the Spirit. His divine presence is a necessity in our journey in the Lord Jesus. In short, the Spirit is the means supplier.

Chapter 3 is "Faith and Repentance." This dynamic duo serves as the activators, used by the Spirit, to transform, the believer. John the Baptist and Jesus' first sermons contain these two ideas: "repent and believe." Repentance and faith are keys to all of the growth patterns in the life of the believer. Without repentance, fellowship cannot be restored to the life of the believer although the relationship through Christ's work on the cross can never be broken. Passages like Psalm 51 and Hebrews 11 will be explored to work through these systemic items and their role in growing and maintaining the spiritual vitality of the believer. We will also look into the life of Jonah and assess the difference between counterfeit and authentic repentance.

The Word of God is an essential means of growth. It is one of the primary ways in which the Lord makes us look like Jesus. In chapter 4 we will delve into the role the Word of God plays in growing us. In connection with the gospel (chapter 1) and the Spirit (chapter 2), it will explain the basic ways that the Word of God calls us to God's Word—the Bible—beginning with the sufficiency of the Word of God in 2 Timothy 2:15; 3:15–17; and 2 Peter 1:19–21. For most of the chapter we will explore our role in taking responsibility in internalizing and applying the Word to our lives. Again it will be rooted in the Spirit leading us into the truth that is in the Word of God as well as how the gospel empowers us to receive the Word of God. Everything from the role of the law, biblical meditation, to believing and hearing the Word, we will see the comprehensive nature by which the Word of God acts as one of the most potent means by which we know God. For without the Word of God we would not have understanding or access to the means in which God has made available to us in order to be transformed. The Word of God is the means by which the worlds were formed and it is the means by which we are. Constant, healthy, and sound contact with the Word of God will be the perfect environment for our continued pursuit of holiness.

In chapter 5, "Prayer," we will talk about how Jesus has given us access to God through His sacrificial death, and how the Father invites us to Himself. We will engage what prayer is, what the sectors of prayer are, the types of prayer, and getting to it. We will survey key prayers of believers in the Bible and church history as a model for how to approach God in prayer. Additionally, we will root prayer in God's sovereignty in connection with our responsibility to do it. God's sovereignty doesn't nullify prayer, but prayer is many times the means by which His will is revealed. The Son intercedes for us while sitting at the right hand of God. The Spirit prays for us when we don't know how to communicate with the God of heaven in hard times.

What is the role of suffering in sanctification? Chapter 6 could be its own book. From Romans chapter 5 to James chapter 1, we will see how the Lord uses trials to expose where we are, where we are not, and where He wants us to be. In addition, we will see this as a gospel pattern in the life of the Christian. We are going into, going through, or coming out of a trial. Trials will be profiled as the Christological pattern of spiritual development in the life of the believer (1 Pet. 2:21). We will explore the various ways in which affliction is a part of our spiritual lives. Our goal would not be to worship suffering or look forward to it, but to utilize those seasons to draw nearer to the Lord and submit to His process of making us look more like the Lord Jesus Christ.

Chapter 7 is all about breaking free from strongholds (2 Cor. 10:3–6). Here we will explore the nature of dealing with the strongholds in our life as a necessity of growth. Without engaging these strongholds, we will not be able to maximize the growth potential that God has for us in the Lord Jesus Christ. We will look at what strongholds are, and how we have been empowered by God to break free from them.

Chapter 8 is about marriage. Martin Luther called marriage the ultimate sanctifier.[1] He talks extensively about the changes that had to take place in his life because of marriage. The Bible itself uses language like *submission* and *sacrifice* to describe the dispositions of a husband and wife. God uses marriage to show both husband and wife their need for the Lord Jesus Christ, and in doing so, the two become helpful to the spiritual growth of the other. Oneness, established in Genesis 2, is realized in Jesus Christ. We will see how the Lord works toward our growth in Him through the crucible of commitment to one another.

Edification is a term used most notably in the corpus of Pauline literature. This means to build up. It also points to the necessity of vital connection to the local church. In chapter 9, "The Local Church and Spiritual Growth"—a.k.a. Community—we will examine passages like Ephesians 4, and will lay out the role of the church as a mutual discipleship community to band together for the maturity of one another. From pastors, deacons, the congregations, missions, evangelism, communion, baptism, the gatherings/community life, giving, preaching and teaching and the "one another's" to church discipline—we will explore the basic ways that God created these to help us to grow. Again these will not be exhaustive, but entry points so that God's people will know the power and role of the church of Jesus Christ that is essential and central to our growth. Matthew 16:18; Hebrews 3:12–15; 10:25–26 will be deep root Scriptures for this chapter.

We will conclude in reflection on *glorification,* and its role in rooting us in the gospel *now.*

My prayer for us is that, as we work through these sections, we will find respite and grace in drawing near to God with confidence that He is conforming us and will conform us to the image of His Son Jesus Christ by faith. In addition, I pray that we would allow the Spirit to use these means of image conformity as we submit to them and grow up into mature believers. ✗

CHAPTER I

Gospel Growth

P aul shows us that we never "get beyond the gospel" in our Christian life.

We never graduate to something more "advanced." The gospel is not the first step in a "stairway of truths"; rather it is more like the hub in a wheel of truth. The gospel is not just the A-B-Cs, but the A–Z of Christianity. The gospel is not just the minimum required doctrine necessary to enter the kingdom, but the way we make all progress in the kingdom.[2]

A young high school basketball player was hungry to go into the League (NBA). You could find him practicing to overcome his weaknesses, both before practice and after. Off-seasons weren't a time to relax but a chance to get better. Lunges, jump shots from every angle, simple layup drills, and other fundamental elements he repeated over and over again, so that when he was in the game he could operate on muscle memory. His passions propelled him into a full scholarship at a major university where he continued to be a beasty athlete. The stats that he was putting on the board were unheard of for a freshman athlete at a school of that magnitude. Soon, NBA scouts, like hawks, began to circle to get him. Everyone wanted to either draft him or have first dibs at him upon graduation.

After arriving in the League, he seemed to have lost his passion for the game. A large contract with guaranteed money became an enabler for laziness. Everyone around him challenged him. He was still one of the top twenty players in the League. But he could have been one of the top three if he retained his high school work ethic. The animal had been tamed by comfort. He became an average player because of average commitment. He needed to remember that the same thing that got him there was the same thing that would keep him there.

Just as his work ethic got this player where he was and would keep him there, so is the gospel to the spiritual life of the believer. The work of Jesus on the cross gets us into a relationship with God, keeps us in a relationship with God, and grows us in our fellowship with God. Faith in the gospel justifies us, secures us, but it will also *grow* us. We are *saved* by grace through faith in Jesus (Eph. 2:8–9) and we are *grown* by the great gospel (Rom. 1:15; 16:25; Gal. 3:3).

One of the most profound verses in the Bible to me on this is Romans 1:15, "So I am eager to preach the gospel to you also who are in Rome." Paul's eagerness to preach the gospel to them isn't because he didn't believe that they had been properly administered the gospel, but because he knows that all of us need to hear the gospel over and over—we never graduate from needing to hear it.

The book of Romans is the most expansive gospel presentation in the Bible. Romans 1:16 speaks of the nature of the gospel, and the rest of the book talks about what the gospel does in the life of the believer. In this book we may see the explicit word *gospel* more than any other book in the Word of God:

Rom. 1:1—Paul, a servant of Christ Jesus, called to be an apostle, set apart for the gospel of God,

Rom. 1:9—For God is my witness, whom I serve with my spirit in the gospel of his Son, that without ceasing I mention you

Rom. 1:15—So I am eager to preach the gospel to you (Christians) also who are in Rome.

Rom. 2:16—on that day when, according to my gospel, God judges the secrets of men by Christ Jesus.

Rom. 10:16—But they have not all obeyed the gospel. For Isaiah says, "Lord, who has believed what he has heard from us?"

Rom. 11:28—As regards the gospel, they are enemies of God for your sake. But as regards election, they are beloved for the sake of their forefathers.

Rom. 15:16—to be a minister of Christ Jesus to the Gentiles in the priestly service of the gospel of God, so that the offering of the Gentiles may be acceptable, sanctified by the Holy Spirit.

Rom. 15:19—by the power of signs and wonders, by the power of the Spirit of God—so that from Jerusalem and all the way around to Illyricum I have fulfilled the ministry of the gospel of Christ

Rom. 15:20—and thus I make it my ambition to preach the gospel, not where Christ has already been named, lest I build on someone else's foundation,

Rom. 16:25—Now to him who is able to strengthen you according to my gospel and the preaching of Jesus Christ,

according to the revelation of the mystery that was kept
✗   secret for long ages

We see that from the prologue to the epilogue/doxology, Paul is gospel-driven. Even in the doxology in Romans 16:25, Paul is wanting the gospel to be what stabilizes the people of God. God makes us durable in the faith for Him. God uses the gospel as the mechanism for growing us.

Think about it like this, a handy man has a tool belt. He is the one ultimately given the credit for the fixing of a sink, toilet, garbage disposal, A/C, or heat. These tools around his belt are the means by which he fixes things for people. The gospel is God's mighty tool belt to fix broken believers.

Galatians 3:3 illustrates that some believers might view their growth outside the realm of gospel and Holy Spirit empowerment. Paul says, "Are you so foolish? Having begun by the Spirit, are you now being perfected by the flesh?" This is something the Galatians were attempting to do, but could not accomplish successfully. Anytime we try and grow without faith in the gospel, we are attempting in the flesh to do only what the Holy Spirit can do in us by faith in the gospel.
✗

What Is Sanctification?

I can remember one of my first experiences in the "Holiness church." They are affectionately called "holy rollers" and "sanctified church." You will never see women wearing pants at church, for example; they believe that we are to wear gender-specific clothing: "A woman shall not wear a man's garment, nor shall a man put on
✗

a woman's cloak, for whoever does these things is an abomination to the LORD your God" (Deut. 22:5). I think they have a point—on some level—here. However, much of their theology is built around the idea of holiness—holiness that is mainly connected to the responsibility of Christians to live holy by radical obedience. What that entails is rooted for them in Hebrews 12:14, "Strive for peace with everyone, and for the holiness without which no one will see the Lord." According to many of my holiness brethren, we have been given power through the work of Christ and the baptism of the Holy Spirit, with evidence such as speaking in tongues, to live holy, and to grow ourselves in that holiness.

By viewing Hebrews 12:14 this way, it can sometimes feel like our holiness rests on us, and that if we don't pursue this holiness, we could lose our relationship with God unless we are "living holy." In other words, our salvation is being kept according to our effort to "be perfect." I am grateful for those in this arena who taught me so much about the foundational truths of the faith. Yet, I found myself wrestling with eternal security, which didn't motivate me to holiness, but by fear, because I believed the security of my salvation was rooted in my ability to "live holy."

The problem with this is that many Christians struggle with this type of structural functional legalism (taken from a class lecture by Bill Lawrence at Dallas Theological Seminary). Most of us see our lives and our sanctification as rooted in *our work for Him* rather than *in what He has done for us.*

As a pastor, this is one of the top three things I help people wrestle with in their souls. There are essentially two types of people I see: (1) Those for whom a shroud covers how they see spiritual growth. They believe spiritual growth comes from their work, not

Christ's, and (2) Those who have a complete lack of wrestling with
holiness at all.

Sanctification Is Being Conformed to the Image of Christ

Sanctification, holiness, Christian growth, spiritual growth, spiritual formation, and *discipleship* are all related terms which all communicate conformity of the *believer* in Jesus Christ to the *image* of Christ. For the life of the believer, there is no other priority but to look like Jesus. Everything in our lives orbits around this reality and must submit itself to God's goals. Romans 8:29 states, "For those whom he foreknew he also predestined to be conformed to the image of his Son, in order that he might be the firstborn among many brothers." On this subject, in my estimation, this is the most important biblical passage to consider. God planned before the foundation of the world that all who would come into a relationship with Him would look like Jesus Christ. Because of the full effort of God we have been, are being, and will be conformed into the image of the Lord Jesus Christ. Accordingly, the goal of God is that the Savior's image will be ours.

There is no team that doesn't possess the desire to win. That is the nature of competition. Failure is not an option, and winning is based on keeping score to achieve a particular goal. Therefore, every team focuses its efforts on building a strategy around how to leverage personnel, resources, and energy. All are systematically focused to win.

Paul writes, "Do you not know that in a race all the runners run, but only one receives the prize? So run that you may obtain it" (1 Cor. 9:24). The prize is why we compete, to win. Even in the winning of a soul to Jesus, the soul is won for discipleship and growth, because to be in Jesus Christ means these things will happen. God's divine plan for the soul of the redeemed is growth. Likewise, 1 Thessalonians 4:3 states, "For this is the will of God, your sanctification: that you abstain from sexual immorality." God's desire is the declared distinction of His people in the world because of our connection to Him. Here it speaks of abstinence from sexual immorality as one of the ways in which this is seen. However, the larger issue is that God has called us to distinction in even our pleasure. Our pleasure should have modesty and depth that guides its application. God's ordained outlets of pleasure should still smell of the holiness that God brought us into Christ to display. He wants us to treat Him as holy, and in doing so, we walk in holiness.

Stages of Sanctification

In his work *An Infinite Journey*, Andrew M. Davis charts the stages of salvation. His stages and many of the verses that he quotes were things that God had already used to help me understand sanctification as a very young disciple, and that helped stabilize my faith. I will borrow from him throughout this section, but nuance his framework in different ways.

Stage 1—The Process of Calling and Drawing: When I was wrestling with eternal security, John's writing in the Bible settled my uncertainty. Through tears, many nights, I found two of the most comforting verses in the Bible: "But I said to you that you have seen me and yet do not believe. All that the Father gives me will come to me, and whoever comes to me I will never cast out" (John 6:36–37). I realized that I was brought to Jesus by God Himself. In other words, I was wooed by the King of kings into a relationship with Jesus Christ as my Savior. I was handed to Jesus by God! Because

God is the one who drew me to Jesus, He will "not never" cast me out; in the Greek, *ou meh* is a double negative. In English a double negative is canceled and thereby becomes a positive—which is why we try to avoid using double negatives. In Greek, however, there is a greater emphasis placed on what is being negated. In other words, when God is the one who brought you to Jesus, "He ain't never gonna let you go." I feel like preaching, right there!

In verses 44, 63, 65, John further explains the process of calling and drawing:

> "No one can come to me unless the Father who sent me draws him. And I will raise him up on the last day." (v. 44)

> "It is the Spirit who gives life; the flesh is no help at all. The words that I have spoken to you are spirit and life." (v. 63)

> And he said, "This is why I told you that no one can come to me unless it is granted him by the Father." (v. 65)

In short, it is the divine initiative of God that draws us into a relationship with Jesus Christ. Human effort is of no consequence for coming to know the living God. Romans 3 speaks of the fact that no one seeks after God. Therefore, it is God who is the seeker; He is not the one who is lost. Our lostness is so deep that we have to be shown it. Born in darkness, only by light do we see our own condition. God illuminates where we are and shows us our need for Him.

> In this drawing process, one encounter after another shapes the heart of the lost person, and though in one sense the unregenerate person is indeed "dead in their transgressions

and sins" (Ephesians 2:1), yet they still live in those sins (Ephesians 2:2) day by day and are experiencing their poisonous effects. Meanwhile, God is putting the pieces together for the moment when at last he will sovereignly give miraculous new life.[3]

Stage 2—The Moment of Regeneration, Faith, and Justification: God then acts upon the hardened heart. He causes us to be born again (1 Pet. 1:3). We will speak of this more directly when we address the role of the Holy Spirit in saving us. "He saved us, not because of works done by us in righteousness, but according to his own mercy, by the washing of regeneration and renewal of the Holy Spirit (Titus 3:5). All at once, when we hear the gospel, we are regenerated. When we repent, and place our faith in the Lord Jesus Christ, because of the act of God causing the preached seed of the Word of God, the gospel transforms our weary souls. God causes us to be cleansed by the blood of Jesus Christ—a heart change takes place. We are convinced of the truth about Christ's death relinquishing God's wrath, our affections are drawn to Jesus, and our will is taken out of bondage to sins and Satan (Ezek. 36:25–27). We believe by the faith provided by God (Rom. 12:3), and are declared righteous by God, having the wrath due us applied to Jesus Christ in our place (Rom. 5:1).

Doesn't all of that make you want to shout in praise to the good Lord? I do. It blows my mind that the Living God eternally organized how He would bring us to Himself. The result of this is that we are united with Christ (2 Cor. 5:17). This union is permanent.

I remember vividly the day I believe that this happened in my own life. It was on the campus of Bowie State University on November 15, 1992. I went to a campus ministry church service and heard the gospel, seemingly, for the first time. I say "seemingly" because all of my interactions with the church up until that point all of a sudden bore special meaning. It all became clear to me. The liturgy of the church—the creeds we recited together, responsive readings, songs of Zion Hymnal, the Gloria Patri, the invocations, benedictions, and doxologies—became clear to me. All of them pointed me to Jesus, and the God who draws used them to draw me to Himself.

In this stage I would add what is sometimes referred to as "definitive" or "positional" sanctification. These terms refer to the same thing. Namely, that God has made us holy through Jesus Christ. Our holiness in Christ, in terms of our standing with God, or position, has been secured through His sacrificial death. Hebrews 10:10 says, "And by that will we have been sanctified through the offering of the body of Jesus Christ once for all." Sanctified is in a *perfect passive participle. Perfect* tense means that our sanctification is a completed work of the past. Consequently, our being set aside as holy by God has been done. *Passive* voice points to the fact that it was done to us, but not by us. *Participle* means that this is a state that describes who we are in terms of identity. Wow! The text adds, "once for all." With our sanctification being something that was done for us forever, we find that our spiritual cleanliness is a done deal.

When a family comes home from the hospital with a new baby, we are sensitive to germs. We wash new clothes before we place them on the baby. Before we administer a bottle to the baby, we have to take it through a sterilization process so that there is nothing unseen that will attack the immune system of the baby. Just as the baby's environment must be cleaned and sterilized, the same has to be done over and over again to our souls. Jesus has eternally sterilized our souls, making us holy. As a result of God's work in Christ for us, we have been set apart for and by God. We have been made suitable for God's purposes.

In the Old Testament, when something is purified by God, that item is no longer the same. That item was viewed as holy and sanctified for the use according to that which the Lord had designated.

> "Then you shall take part of the blood that is on the altar, and of the anointing oil, and sprinkle it on Aaron and his garments, and on his sons and his sons' garments with him. He and his garments shall be holy, and his sons and his sons' garments with him." (Exod. 29:21)

The same is true for us. Prior to contact with Christ, we were common vessels. But because of contact with Christ and the Spirit, we are now "vessels of mercy" (Rom. 9:23). This distinction marks our existence forever. When I dated my wife, as much as I would like to have said she was "mine," she wasn't. And I was not hers. However, upon marrying her, we "officially," in the eyes of God, belonged to one another (Gen. 2:23–24; Song of Sol. 6:3; 1 Cor. 7). We were definitively set apart, exclusively reserved for one another.

Stage 3—The Process of Sanctification: As we have seen already, our sanctification has been secured by Jesus. We are positionally sanctified and made holy by the Lord. However, in our everyday life, we don't often function in the holiness God has granted. For instance, when a child is born, he or she is born fully human and is as human as they ever are going to be. On the other hand, being a newborn human, babies are unable to maximize their full potential. Walking, talking, eating on one's own, etc.—all of the potential for these things exist in the child, but development is necessary for potential to become realized. Believers are viewed as spiritual babes when we are born again. First Peter 2:2 and Hebrews 5:11–6:2 call us to be nurtured by milk, or elementary teaching about Jesus, when we are newborn. However, we are not called to remain as newborns; we are called to press on to maturity.

In His humanity Jesus experienced both natural and spiritual growth (Luke 2:52; Heb. 5:7–10). If Jesus grew spiritually, how much more do we need to grow? He became human while remaining God and grew in His humanity. His deity needed no growth; His human soul, although perfect, grew—mind-blowing!

In sum, sanctification in the New Testament is seen as "a one-time event and as a process, the believers being and becoming holy and acting correspondingly."[4] When Jesus returns and fully glorifies us in Him, we will be fully sanctified (2 Thess. 1:12). Sanctification is the ongoing process that removes the pollution of sin and gradually conforms the sinner to the image of Christ (Eph. 4:20–24). The sinner's justification definitively sets the believer apart from the world of sin and God always looks upon him as holy because of the imputed righteousness of Christ.[5] In our lives, sanctification is God's dynamic process that moves a disciple along in practical holiness. The same way we are saved is the same way we are kept. We are justified by faith in Christ and we are sanctified by faith in Christ. In this we are becoming progressively more submissive to God. In God's economy, we are to be in a passionate chase after Him.

God's Work and Our Responsibility

We must understand very clearly that sanctification is rooted in what God has done for us in Jesus Christ. Sanctification is a work initiated by and continued by God. It is not God starting the engine and then letting us drive. But it is God who is the starter and the driving force of our relationship with Him. We are sanctified by the Spirit. It is His activity within the Godhead that causes us to be born again, stay born again, grow in our new birth, and be with Jesus (2 Thess. 2:13; 1 Pet. 1:2).

Sanctification must not be seen as separate from the gospel but a part of it. Progressive sanctification isn't a separate process from justification, but an extension of it. God's saving work may be tightly tied to our growth. For it is by His transformational work in the gospel whereby our commitment to grow is rooted. That is why Romans 5, 6, 7, and 8 work in sequence. They display the glorious journey of the believer in Christ. Chapter 5 is the announcement of the coronation of our justification by faith in Jesus, and our familial transference from the old Adam. Romans 6 shows us that we experienced the excitement of conversion, and must develop a healthy understanding of grace. In developing a healthy understanding of grace, we take what Christ has done for us seriously and soak in the death, burial, and resurrection. Next, in chapter 7, we see that our life is a wrestle with the old self, and that we are in a pattern of brokenness and failure. Consequently, we worship Christ Jesus for deliverance from the old self. Whereas chapter 7 focuses on the internal struggle of sanctification, chapter 8 points to the external items which make for a hostile, albeit fertile environment for God to sanctify us.

Purification is the basis of sanctification. By his sovereign action in Christ, God sets apart and binds to himself those who have been purified from the defilement of sin. This objective, consecrating work of God has profound implications for the attitude and behavior of those who believe.

Under the terms of that covenant, God writes his law in the hearts and minds of all his people, enabling them to know him and serve him in a new way. Such dedication to God is made possible by the sacrifice which allows him to "remember their sins and their lawless deeds no more" (cf. 10:17–18). As in Jeremiah's promise, so in Hebrews, a once-for-all forgiveness of sins is the basis of a new commitment to God on the part of his people.[6]

What has been done for us in Christ enables and empowers God's goals for our lives. Our motivation for growth comes from God.

A rich father was worried about the entitlement that his children could develop growing up in such a wealthy home. Being brought up in an environment where your dad is a billionaire could develop a sense of entitlement that, if left unchecked, would become toxic. In the mind of this father, all that he had belonged to his children, but he wanted them to have the maturity and wisdom necessary to steward all that would be given to them. At times, they were frustrated that he would not buy them everything that they wanted, when they wanted it. He made them work, and work hard. It wasn't that he was making them work for their inheritance—because it was already theirs—but he wanted to help them to grow so that they could handle what was already going to be given to them.

Our inheritance of sanctification works the same way. Our sanctification is already ours, but God calls us to strive, fight, and connect to the means that He has provided for us to mature. These are mechanisms He uses to grow us. In the area of progressive sanctification, this tells the story of how our growth happens. On the one hand, it is our responsibility to pursue holiness, yet God is the one who actually causes the growth to be a reality.

I believe that in different stages of my ministry I have preached faith-based *justification,* but works-based *sanctification.* What do I mean by this? I wrestled with understanding that the whole of our salvation is a total work of God—not just our regeneration. To be honest, I still wrestle with recognizing that the means that God uses to sanctify us isn't us growing ourselves, but God graciously growing us in light of our active commitment to Him. In all fairness, I'm in the middle of trying to understand my sanctification, in believing that it is God who does this—and I know I'm not alone.

In Philippians 2:12–13 Paul makes a paradoxical statement in regards to our growth,

> Therefore, my beloved, as you have always obeyed, so now, not only as in my presence but much more in my absence, work out your own salvation with fear and trembling, for it is God who works in you, both to will and to work for his good pleasure.

Paul calls the Philippian church to obedience motivated by God's work in them—not Paul's presence with them. Paul wanted them to know that he doesn't work in them, but God does. In their pursuit of holiness, he calls them to work *out* their salvation, not *for* their salvation.

Salvation in the New Testament is a word based on context that can refer to *justification* (being declared righteous by faith in Jesus), *sanctification* (the position and process of growing in faith and holiness in Jesus), or *glorification* (the consummation of our identity in Jesus). Here it is clear that Paul is speaking about *sanctification*. We are called to "work out your own salvation."

One commentator says it well:

> To work out or bring about one's own salvation is different in meaning from the admonition of [Philippians] 2:4, where the readers are encouraged to place the interests of others before their own. The apostle is thus not contradicting his earlier instructions.[7] ἑαυτῶν σωτηρίαν κατεργάζεσθε is a demand to make that salvation fruitful in the here and now[8] as the graces of Christ or the fruit of the Spirit (Gal. 5:22–23) are produced in their lives. It involves continually living in a manner worthy of the gospel of Christ (Phil. 1:27) or "the continual translating into action of the principles of the gospel that they had believed."[9] Paul has in mind a *"continuous, sustained, strenuous effort,"* which is elsewhere described under the imagery of a pursuit, a following after, a pressing on, a contest, a fight, or a race (Phil. 3:12; cf. Rom. 14:19; 1 Cor. 9:24–27; 1 Tim. 6:12).[10] Further, to speak of believers being responsible for the outworking of their personal salvation in their day-to-day living in no way denies that this σωτηρία is an act of God. . . . In precisely the same way "make your calling and election sure" (2 Pet. 1:10 KJV) does not suggest that election is not God's act.[11]

Our effort to do this comes from God. Even our work is God's. Colossians 1:29 says it best: "For this I toil, struggling with all his energy that he powerfully works within me." In addition, the context earlier instructs us not to look out for our own interest but the interest of others, then states, work out your own salvation. The impact of a gospel community filled with gospel-driven sanctification on the individual level always has a corporate effect.

In 2 Peter 1, this idea rings true as well. We are to furnish our faith with moral excellence, knowledge, self-control, steadfastness, godliness (all internal), then brotherly affection (body life), to love (missional engagement).

"Own" points to the personal responsibility we all have on an individual level to pursue holiness. Paul exhorts Timothy to be responsible in seeking godliness and holiness (1 Tim. 4). This is an empowered ownership, as you will see. In Titus 2:11–13, Paul cites grace as the motivation for our pursuit of spiritual growth in between the two advents of Jesus Christ in this present age. God graciously instructs us to chase Him.

David Peterson puts it this way:

> Since Jesus Christ is the revealed truth and power of godliness (cf. 1 Tim. 3: 16), to exercise in godliness is "to work out one's salvation according to the power of Christ who works within" (Knight 1992:200; cf. Phil. 2:12–13). Put another way, Titus 2:11–12 asserts that "the grace of God has appeared, bringing salvation to all, training us to renounce impiety [Gk. *asebeian*] and worldly passions, and in the present age to live lives that are self-controlled, upright, and godly [Gk. *eusebōs*]" (NRSV). Here the coming

of Christ is viewed as the ultimate manifestation of the grace of God. He not only provides eternal salvation but "instructs" or "disciplines" us (Gk. *paideuousa*, cf. Heb. 12:5–11) to renounce evil and live in a way that pleases him. The motivation for change and the power to live differently come from believing in the gospel about his grace (Titus 2:11–14), and experiencing the regenerating and renewing work of his Spirit (3:3–7).[12]

Back in Philippians 2:12 we see the posture with which we are to seek holiness, "fear and trembling." Interesting word combination for something that is supposed to be by grace, through faith. As we take a deeper look into these words, we recognize that Paul uses this idiom in other places (1 Cor. 2:3; 2 Cor. 7:15; Eph. 6:5; Phil. 2:12). Each instance is in the context of some sort of gospel transformation. Moreover, the statement isn't speaking of fear as other instances throughout this Scripture contextually point to. Here it is speaking of our gospel disposition in sanctification. This is a hyper-potent communication of awe and reverence for the Lord and His gospel. In essence this phrase means to stand in profound awe of the reality of God and the gospel. In awe of God we bow our lives to Him now as an expression of worship in our daily lives, knowing that we will bow to the good Lord later (v. 10). It isn't about a fear of not getting things right, but a worshipful thankfulness with the fact that we get to live for Christ through the power of Christ.

Becoming a father is one of the weightiest, yet awe-inspiring opportunities that has come into my life. My awe of God, giving me my children as gifts to steward, motivates me every day to invest in them as long as they are with me. Words can't express my passion for them to live for Jesus. So I repent before them, and seek to love the Lord and point them toward Him. As God has saved two of them, and as we wait for God to save the next one, I'm at a loss for words at my gratitude for the work of God and utilizing my parenting as a roadmap to the cross. That awe is that which with, I believe, verse 12 is pregnant.

. . . *for it is God who works in you.* What a statement. God's work within us sums it up. Our motivation to work is God's work, and the work in full is God's work. In Ephesians 2:10 we are called, "his workmanship." Being God's workmanship points to the shaping work of the living God as overseer and superintendent of our sanctification. God the Holy Spirit is the one active, implementing every aspect of our salvation. As seen in our earlier mention of Colossians 1:29, the energizing for us to work is from God.

. . . *both to will and to work for His good pleasure.* It is God who furnishes us with the desire through renewed affections to want to grow. Hence, when we sense our lack of growth, the Lord nurtures our appetite for Him. It takes God to desire God. Being awestruck *before* God comes *from* God, for it is He who gives us the ability to have a finite glimpse of Him and His great gospel. Our work for Him comes from His empowerment.

When my sons don't want to obey, to jump-start their obedience I provide an incentive to motivate them to the task. And sometimes, as they are working, they actually begin to *enjoy* the work, regardless of the source of initial motivation. God's gospel stirs desire in us, which leads to our working—through *His* strength, on *His* desired goals for *our* lives. And like my boys, sometimes we find that we enjoy the work along the way.

Why All the Fuss?

My reason for hammering away at this issue is so we might recognize that it is the Lord who grows us by faith in the gospel, in submission to His means. We have the tendency to trace the good in our lives back to ourselves. But in the end, we find that it is all a work of God.

My hope is, as we transition our thinking, to see that the means of growth in our lives—as we suffer, read and study the Word, pray, fight for our marriages, walk in godly singleness and supernatural self-control—are a gift from God. The result will be that God unleashes a power in our lives never before seen. ✗

CHAPTER 2

The Holy Spirit's Role in Our Growth

Great men receive tremendous credit for their accomplishment—from presidents to civil rights leaders to pastors. Little do most of us know, however, that without the impact of a supportive wife, there wouldn't be the grounding necessary to enable leaders to create movements. Would John Adams have been the president he was without Abigail? Would Martin Luther King have been the man with impact without Coretta? Who would Billy Graham be without Ruth? It is baffling how little credit wives receive in regards to the great movements in the world. God's Word calls wives the indispensable companion. In other words, what could we do without them?

I would also suggest the eternal Helper—the Holy Spirit—is treated as a silent partner in our growth who rarely gets the credit and glory He rightly deserves for the application of the gospel in our lives. We tend to err in this regard in one of two ways.

First, for too long the church (in different sectors) has had a reductionistic view of the Holy Spirit. In many cases He is relegated to being understood simply as an idea from the Bible. We have ignored and therefore disconnected ourselves from the power of the Holy Spirit.

On the other hand, the Holy Spirit has been used as the means for triumphalism and abuses disconnected from God's Word. This is also a reductionistic view. The Holy Spirit becomes a sort of shorthand for all of the gifts and power the Spirit provides, without the rule of God over those gifts; instead, we prop ourselves up over those gifts instead of God through His Word.

Both are equal and sad extremes that need to be corrected. He is the member of the Godhead who is lied about most. People say that He says and is doing things He is not. Or they ascribe things to Him that is obviously far from His holy character.

We all need a more robust bandwidth of who the Spirit is and what He does. In addition, we need to connect with Him by faith in Jesus. A. W. Pink said:

> The need for this is real and pressing, for ignorance of the Third Person of the Godhead is most dishonoring to Him, and highly injurious to ourselves. The late George Smeaton of Scotland began his excellent work upon the Holy Spirit by saying, "Wherever Christianity has been a living power, the doctrine of the Holy Spirit has uniformly been regarded, equally with the Atonement and Justification by faith, as the article of a standing or falling church. The

distinctive feature of Christianity as it addresses itself to man's experience, is the work of the Spirit, which not only elevates it far above all philosophical speculation, but also above every other form of religion."[13]

Many of us (including myself) feel at a loss in recognizing the Person (who He is) and identifying role (what He does) of the Spirit in our lives. We must commit greater attention to this area. As we grow in our understanding of the Spirit, we can pray accordingly—everything about our prayer life will change. My hope is that, for our churches, the Spirit will rise in our hearts above being a mystical specter to sovereign God who rules over our souls.

Not at all too strong was the language of Samuel Chadwick when he said, "The gift of the Spirit is the crowning mercy of God in Christ Jesus. It was for this all the rest was. The Incarnation and Crucifixion, the Resurrection and Ascension were all preparatory to Pentecost. Without the gift of the Holy Spirit all the rest would be useless. The great thing in Christianity is the gift of the Spirit. The essential, vital, central element in the life of the soul and the work of the Church is the Person of the Spirit" (*Joyful News*, 1911).[14]

How quickly we forget that He was the means by which Mary conceived the Lord Jesus. This is why in gospel-centered theology we must not forget the Spirit: because He is the one who applies to us every component of the gospel. Without the Holy Spirit there would be no connection to God. Therefore, we must take some time and speak of His glorious role in our journey with God the Father through Jesus Christ in Sanctification.

We Need to Need God (Holy Spirit)

In our Western culture, there is an overemphasis on self-achievement. We so esteem people that are "self-made." In other words, we reward people who seem to need no one, save their ability to accomplish insurmountable life goals. We find that some are so steeped in self-achievement that they are almost awarded a divine status. Whether it's an athlete, businessperson, or artist, we are suckers for self-starting and self-motivated over-achievers.

However, if you take a closer look, in so many cases you will find a different story. You will find a multitude of people that, without whom, every award, every trophy, every position of leadership would be impossible. We see it in our heroes' failures as well. Look at our athletes who, over the years, have had to forfeit their achievements because of illegal performance-enhancing substances they used to achieve the impossible. We never achieve anything worthwhile on our own; the "self-made man" is a myth.

The pressure to be perceived this way makes its way into so many sectors of society, even into the matrix of the people of God. As Christians, we may not say it, but we have symptoms of the same disease. Rather than bragging about natural talent, we boast in spiritual gifts. Rather than concert stages, we pump our pulpits for all they are worth. The fact is we, as the church, do it too; we just veil it in different language.

But in God's economy, God seems to reward the needy who respond to Him, and become diligent because of Him. The greatest people that God used in the Bible were all marked by their inability to accomplish anything without the Lord. Moses didn't want to lead the people of God one step without His empowering presence. Gideon, being the least in all of Israel, only found strength in His divine presence. David was nothing until God's divine presence was upon him. Even the Lord of Glory, in the incarnation, didn't begin His ministry until He was clothed with the Spirit (at His baptism). In the Psalms, God-neediness is rewarded with close proximity of the divine presence (Pss. 34 and 51). In Haggai, God had to promise the people of God over and over that He would be with them through the promised Spirit.[15] We need to need the Spirit!

Don't get me wrong, we must utilize and maximize what has been placed under our authority, as those who are under Christ's authority. Yet we must not for one minute think our ingenuity, left to itself, could accomplish heaven's agenda. We need the power of the Holy Ghost—wind that turns the turbines of our souls, lives, families, and ministries. Our sanctification is no different. He is the One whom we must long to be noticeably present in all of our lives. I'm not speaking of some spooky guessing game of false mysticism, but the unspeakable reality that nothing that is too big for us—which includes more than you estimate, whatever you think—would ever happen by human strength, only by the Spirit's enablement.

Remember Zerubbabel: "Not by might, nor by power, but by my Spirit, says the LORD of hosts" (Zech. 4:6). He is indispensable and necessary for all of our life and growth. We don't need the Spirit because He is codependent on us, or has a need to be needed, but because in Him we live, move, and have our being.

The Spirit Is the Midwife of the New Birth

Gives us everything we need for life and godliness (2 Pet. 1:3). I am a foodie! I love "farm to table" restaurants and dives. The reason I like them is that they take special care to make sure everything is fresh and properly delivered to those in the restaurant. In addition, they support local farmers by getting their fresh resources to the customer. Although not specifically stated in this passage, but true of the corpus of the Scripture, the Spirit supplies us with the resources of the kingdom through Jesus. He delivers the fresh resources of heaven to the parched table of our hearts and lives. Everything that we need for life and godliness is given to us in order that we may be able to fight sin. This is very encouraging for us. Everything that God requires of us, He has provided in Jesus and practically accomplishes it through the Spirit. It is clear that in 1 Corinthians 2:13–14 it is the Spirit who helps us understand the things that have been freely given us in Jesus.

We would not be in the faith without the Spirit. Titus 3:5 shows us that our justification in Christ is applied by the Spirit. It is the Spirit who washes us with the blood of the Lamb of God. He scrubs our filthy souls with the blood of Jesus until they turn from death to life. The Spirit does His work as a masterful homebuilder who is meticulous about the condition of a house. God acts upon us, in the gospel, through the Spirit.

The Spirit orchestrates the preaching of the gospel (Acts 16:9–10; Rom. 10:14–15). Every time the gospel is preached, it is a work of the Holy Spirit. Throughout the book of Acts, the Holy Spirit is the one who formulates moments for gospel preachers and lost hearers to hear the good news about Jesus. One of the reasons why my ministry is dedicated to church planting is because it is the means through which the Spirit has filled the earth since the resurrection. But even the most skilled church-planting strategists are impotent without the power of the Spirit to orchestrate the work.

Is there any believer that wouldn't affirm that the moment of their salvation wasn't a Holy Ghost appointment?

As I have already said, for me it was November 15, 1992, on the campus of Bowie State University. I was spiritually exhausted and went to a service with a girl that I liked. We sat with each other and heard the Word of God. I haven't been the same since that great day; it was the most important day of my life. God saved me and led me out of my lifelessness into the abundant life. It is clear to me that I was supposed to be there.

Jesus quotes Isaiah 61:1–2a, which points to the fact that one of the reasons the Spirit was placed on Him at baptism was to preach the gospel. Jesus' ministry was driven by divine moments, orchestrated by the Spirit, for preaching of the gospel to the lost of heart. Even when we look at the Ethiopian eunuch, Philip was taken there by the Spirit and moved on by the Spirit. The whole of the experience of hearing and believing in the gospel belongs to the Spirit's power. Here are a few ways the Spirit works in that process:

- We are convicted of sin righteousness and judgment (John 16:8–11).
- We have our hearts opened to the gospel to confess Jesus (1 Cor. 12:3).
- We are regenerated and renewed by the Spirit through the gospel (Titus 3:5).

- He seals and secures us in the faith (Eph. 1:14; 1 Pet. 1:5).
- And of course, as we will see throughout *Unleashed,* He causes us to grow into conformity to the image of Christ.

One the most difficult parts of being a parent is helping children navigate the world in light of the truth of the gospel. Because, let's face it, it's difficult for us to navigate the world in that manner, let alone helping our children do the same. From cartoons, to movies, to toys, the stories they read, to what they learn from friends, school and family members—it is always a delicate balance of figuring out how to communicate the truth to them while combating the things that could become harmful if the seeds of falsehood are allowed to grow.

I watch cartoons with my sons, play video games with them, and even frequent the comic shop to be there as a buffer when they are carried along by all the fun. I didn't realize, until I had children of my own, how much they are being indoctrinated. So much of what is in all of these means of entertainment seeks to provide them with a worldview. All of these "positive" outlets have an agenda for my children—for all of our children. The question for me, as I enter into their world with them, isn't, "What's their agenda?" but, "What's mine?" As a father, I am vested in what their hearts believe. My desire for their journey is that the truth of the gospel, through the power of the Spirit, would cause them to see Jesus and His Word clearly, that they would walk with, know, and love the living God from their youth. Therefore, I want to lead them through the world into truth.

Jesus, in the upper-room discourse (John 14–17), is so concerned with the spiritual formation of His disciples that He promises that

He will send the Spirit to pick up where He left off, in order to make sure that God's people are led into truth. This is why the Holy Spirit is called the Spirit of Truth. When we think about truth, sometimes we think about it as merely correct information, or a non-lie. But truth is not merely correct information; truth is a Person (John 14:6). The Spirit is leading us into a deeper sense of who Jesus Christ is, which involves both information and transformation.

Being led into truth about Jesus leads to a greater awareness of who He is so that we can experience freedom (John 8:31–32).

(1) When the Holy Spirit comes, he will *guide* the disciples *into all truth*. What Jesus had said in 8:31–32, "If you continue to follow my teaching you are really my disciples, and you will know the truth, and the truth will set you free," will ultimately be realized in the ongoing ministry of the Holy Spirit to the disciples after Jesus' departure. (2) The things the Holy Spirit speaks to them will not be things which originate from himself (*he will not speak on his own authority*), but things he has heard. This could be taken to mean that no new revelation is involved, as R. E. Brown does (*John* [AB], 2:714–15). This is a possible but not a necessary inference. The point here concerns the source of the things the Spirit will say to the disciples and does not specifically exclude originality of content. (3) Part at least of what the Holy Spirit will reveal to the disciples will concern *what is to come,* not just fuller implications of previous sayings of Jesus and the like. This does seem to indicate that at least some new revelation is involved. But the Spirit is not the source or originator of these things—Jesus is the source,

and he will continue to speak to his disciples through the
Spirit who has come to indwell them.[16]

✗

This leads me to believe that His role is to push us toward
maturity in Jesus. Being led into truth points to being a motivating
source for someone's actions. Hence, we will be escorted by the Holy
Spirit into a deeper sense of who Jesus is. Because the Spirit searches
the depths of God (1 Cor. 2:10), and Jesus shares in that, He will take
of what He knows about God in Christ and lead us into a deeper
connection to whom Jesus is. As this happens it will strengthen our
fellowship with Him.

One time I went to a concert for free because I was given
complimentary tickets by the artist. I was also invited to come
backstage to spend more time with the artist. However, in order
to get backstage, someone from his crew had to meet me at a
designated place and escort me into the back where he was located.
The Holy Spirit is our escort into greater intimacy in the presence
of Christ.

Our entire spiritual life as disciples is the Spirit progressively
making the Savior known to us. In light of this, our goal in life must
center around the goal of the Spirit: to know truth in Jesus more
intimately by faith. As the Spirit leads us into this deeper intimacy,
it will not be for us just to revel in that divine presence, but to be
motivated for a great commitment to gospel mission in the world.
Paul prays toward this end in Ephesians 1:15–23 for us to be deeply
illuminated.

Being led into truth about Jesus is the primary ministry of the
Holy Spirit. From leading us to faith in Jesus Christ, to initially
saving us, maintaining our faith in Jesus Christ as He sanctifies us,

and preserving our faith in the blessed hope that He will glorify us—my hope is that this is not an over-simplification of the Holy One's role in our lives, but an appropriate, gospel-centered view of Him.

Grows Us in Identifying with Jesus

Fake I.D. cards were a big thing back in the day. Underage teens used to get these made in order to get into places where they were not authorized to be. These cards contained falsified information on it about the person so that those who saw it would be led to believe things about the person's identity that was not authentic. A legitimate identification card would communicate a person's identity reliably. The I.D. could then be used to gain both privileges and responsibilities associated with their identity. For example, a twenty-one-year-old, verified by their I.D. card, can gain access to most places in the city that have an age requirement for entry but warrant civil service, like jury duty or military drafts. While teenagers who use fake I.D. cards want all of the privileges associated with having a different—often times older—identity, they seldom want any of the responsibilities. That is due to a lack of maturity, and the need for growth.

Jesus makes it clear that God gets greatest glory out of our lives when we bear much fruit. The fruit of the Spirit is the I.D. card of the fact that we are in a relationship with Jesus Christ. They are called the fruit of the Spirit because they are given to us at salvation by the Spirit as components of our sanctification that we possess and will be grown in for a lifetime. Peter uses a similar list in 1 Peter 1. However, in Galatians 5:22–23, this list is given as a measure of how our growth is charted as we grow in the gospel by faith. Love, joy, peace, patience, kindness, goodness, faithfulness, gentleness, and self-control are all fundamental points of what it means to walk in the Spirit. As the Spirit grows us, the fruit of the Spirit in all its components are to be ever increasing. As we begin to transition to the other section of this resource, we will see how God the Spirit uses a multitude of means of grace in our life to grow in the Lord. Like an I.D. card, the fruit of the Spirit bears with it all of the privileges and responsibilities of life in Christ.

Filling of the Spirit

"What in the world does it mean to be filled with the Spirit?" is not an altogether bad question—many godly people disagree about its meaning. Also, how does it relate to our growth in God? You can survey multiple Christian tribes and find the Spirit's filling is reduced to either one of two things: *spiritual gifts or right living.* Both have their place, but I would define the Spirit's ongoing filling of the believer as a sign of submission and spiritual growth in Jesus.

Ephesians 5:18–20 is where we go for our dim eyes to see the reality of the filling of the Spirit clearly:

> And do not get drunk with wine, for that is debauchery, but be filled with the Spirit, addressing one another in psalms and hymns and spiritual songs, singing and making melody to the Lord with your heart, giving thanks always and for everything to God the Father in the name of our Lord Jesus Christ.

We see glimmers of this in the Old Testament (OT), but we first see the phraseology in this sense in the New Testament (NT) when the angel came to Zechariah stating that John the Baptist would be filled with the Spirit in the womb. Another occasion was when Elizabeth was filled with the Spirit when Mary came into her house. We see it in Acts 2 with the full arrival of the Spirit upon the church, and the filling of the Spirit as a sign of God being with His people.[17] All of these are powerful instances and important examples, but Ephesian 5:18 helps us to understand the nature and purpose of being filled with the Spirit.

Be filled with the Holy Spirit is a command. That means we are, in some way, supposed to seek being filled with the Spirit actively. However, it is in the passive voice, which means it is something that happens *to us,* not *by us.* Present tense points to the fact that it should be a constant pursuit of the believer.

In looking in to the broader context of Ephesians, we see that Paul calls for us to "know the love of Christ that surpasses knowledge, that you may be filled with all the fullness of God" (3:19). We are to be filled with the fullness of God. We are to be filled *by means of the Spirit.* That is, the Spirit of God is the means by which we are filled with the fullness of God. God the Spirit grows our souls in submission to the Godhead. Moreover, it is rooted in the love of Christ.

Therefore, the filling of the Spirit is the constant funneling of the life of Christ into the practical life of the believer. As Jesus stated, the Spirit will take what is Christ's and dispense it to us. "The author [Paul] then brings his argument to a crescendo in 5:18: Believers are to be filled *by* Christ *by means of* the Spirit *with* the content of the fullness of God."[18] In essence, the Spirit is filling us with God.

In the light of these earlier instances of the "fullness" language, then, we conclude that the *content* with which believers have been (or are being) filled is the fullness of (the triune) God or of Christ. No other text in Ephesians (or elsewhere in Paul) *focuses* specifically on the Holy Spirit as the *content* of this fullness. It is better, then, to understand 5:18 in terms of the Spirit's mediating the fullness of God and Christ to believers.[19] In other words, Paul's readers are to be transformed by the Spirit into the likeness of God and Christ, ideas which are entirely consistent with the earlier exhortations of 4:32–5:2. Significantly, as we have seen, it is only in this passage of Ephesians that believers are urged to be imitators of God (5:1). To be admonished, "Be filled by the Spirit," then, means that Paul's readers are urged to let the Spirit change them more and more into the image of God and Christ, a notion which is consistent with Pauline theology elsewhere.[20]

With this emphasis being made a bit clearer, we must see the filling of the Spirit as essential to the comprehensive spiritual formation of the believer. This means we must not relegate this to moralism. Nor should we reduce it to the use of spiritual gifts. Our spiritual growth demands that we be filled with the Spirit, in obedience to the Word of God (Eph. 5:18). We see based on 3:19 and 5:18–20, and several Acts passages that being filled comes through (but isn't limited to) corporate worship, prayer, mission, and preaching—all by faith in the gospel. We see in Acts 4:31 that the church prayed and were filled with the Spirit and spoke the word of God with boldness. On the day of Pentecost, they were praying and were filled. We see that Peter (Acts 4:8) and Paul (13:9) were filled with the Spirit in the context of mission. What is remarkable about each instance is that no one filled themselves, but the Spirit filled them in the midst of activities of faith. This is how the righteous live by faith.

As we compare Luke-Acts to Ephesians, there is both continuity and discontinuity between the two, as it relates to being filled by the Spirit. On the one hand, we see in both that being filled with the Spirit is a constant condition in the life of the believer that should be sought. On the other hand, we see what I will call "Spirit-filled moments." These moments are key points by which the Spirit is said to fill the believer at that particular moment, for a particular purpose. When Jesus promises the disciples that they will receive power when the Holy Ghost comes upon them, the purpose was so that they would become effective witnesses. And like the disciples in the NT, we share the same multifaceted mission arising out of the presence of the Spirit in our lives as believers. Sanctification and mission—Ferguson affirms this dual reality as well. The Spirit fills us to propel us on His mission, for His purposes.

> Luke-Acts speaks of being filled with or being full of the Spirit as an ongoing condition, but also describes particular occasions when individuals appear to experience distinct fillings. . . . To be filled with the Spirit refers predominantly to exhibiting the fruit of the Spirit in a life that is under the Lordship of the Spirit (cf. Eph. 5:18). But the latter occasions refer to special influx of ability and power in the service of the kingdom. This is what is in view in Acts 1:8 and evidenced in Acts 2:4. Interestingly this seems to be invariably

related to the speech of those whom the Spirit fills. They receive "power" to be Christ's witnesses.[21]

✗

Conclusion

In looking more deeply into the glorious filling, we see that the filling of the Spirit is to be filled with the Godhead. In essence, the Spirit is the means by which the communicable attributes[22] of God and/or the fruit of the Spirit is nurtured and developed in us that we may look more like Christ. Love, joy, peace, patience, kindness, gentleness, faithfulness, and self-control are all ours through the Spirit, but He lives to fill us with them. They become more ours as we are in pursuit of growing in them. In all of the areas in which we will explore throughout the duration of this work, we grow in this in and through everything from marriage to suffering. In the rest of the chapters, we will see some of the means that the Spirit uses to fill us with God and make us look more like Jesus.

Go. Be filled with the Spirit. Unleash His power in your life for the purpose of His mission. ✗

CHAPTER 3

Faith and Repentance

I consider myself a pound cake aficionado. I enjoy the crustiness of the top, fresh out of the oven, as well as the moist interior. There isn't anything like a freshly baked pound cake to bless the soul. My wife and I went to some folks' home and had a delectable meal. Upon dessert being served, to my surprise, but not to my dismay, it was pound cake.

It came fresh out of the oven and I was ready to be anointed by its presence. However, upon reception of this delight on my tongue, something was deeply wrong.

I asked our host what type of cake it was again. They replied, "Pound cake." They then said, "Oh yeah, you recognize the difference?"

In my mind, I'm like, *YES!*

They said, "Yes, we substituted out the pound of butter for applesauce."

I felt like I had been bamboozled. You see, pound cake isn't pound cake without the pound of butter. I want it at least once or twice a year—not too often. And when I do have it, I want the real deal. Without knowing it, my host didn't realize that in changing that one ingredient the identity of the cake changed from pound cake to just cake.

Just as this one ingredient impacted that pound cake, if one ingredient of the gospel is removed, it would change the identity of what we believe. If you take repentance or faith out of the gospel, the integrity of what we say we profess has been altered. The true gospel itself cannot be changed by man, but if one of the ingredients is removed, the gospel we say we believe goes from being the Good News to just empty philosophy.

Faith and repentance are two key ingredients of what is required to receive the gospel and to grow in it. Our spiritual growth can be stunted if we aren't repenting of our sin and believing in Christ's work on our behalf to plant and sustain us.

What Is Repentance?

One of my favorite songs in the world is "Running Back to You" by Commissioned. The song relates to a person that has been out in the world and the great God drawing that person back to Him. It is an ode to repentance. Get online; go listen to it.

In college, I could remember smoking a drug in my car while driving. A Christian friend gave me a cassette tape with a ton of Christian songs on it. I was a believer, but I wrestled with a ton of issues. While in the car, I pressed Play without knowledge of what I was doing. I heard these lyrics and began to weep bitterly. I sensed my need to repent. This song was a major component that the Lord used to call me to repentance. This, and so many other key moments, are what the Lord used to place me on an intentional sanctifying trajectory.

Repentance may be defined as the conscious turning [of the regenerate person] away from sin and toward God in a complete change of living, which reveals itself in a new way of thinking, feeling, and willing (modified from authors Hoekema and Watson). Literally a change of mind—not about individual plans, intentions, or beliefs, but rather a change in the whole person from a sinful course of action to God. Repentance is both edifying and evangelistic, ministerial and missional, worship and a witness. Here are some other helpful definitions:

1. To feel remorse, contrition, or self-reproach for what one has done or failed to do; be contrite.
2. To feel such regret for past conduct as to change one's mind regarding it: *repented of intemperate behavior.*
3. To make a change for the better as a result of remorse or contrition for one's sins.[23]

In the NT, repentance primarily relates to the Greek words *metanoéō* and *metńoia*, which mean to understand something differently after thinking it over. This change of mind necessarily leads to changed actions, in keeping with the Greek view that the mind (*noús*) controls the body. Repentance comprises a central theme in the preaching of Jesus, Peter, and Paul.[24]

Charles Spurgeon, the lion of London, the prince of preachers, said the following on the topic of repentance:

I learn from the Scriptures that repentance is just as necessary to salvation as faith is, and the faith that has not repentance going with it will have to be repented of.

Repentance is as much a mark of a Christian, as faith
is. A very little sin, as the world calls it, is a very great sin to
a true Christian.[25]

Jesus' first sermon was connected to one of John the Baptist's
sermons. Jesus says, "Now after John was arrested, Jesus came into
Galilee, proclaiming the gospel of God, and saying, 'The time is
fulfilled, and the kingdom of God is at hand; repent and believe in
the gospel'" (Mark 1:14–15).

Jesus communicated that He wanted people to change their
minds about their lives, what God is like, His kingdom, and namely
His Messiah's coming. He wanted them to embrace His viewpoint.
Repentance is the work of God by which He (through the Spirit)
acts upon the sinner so that we may see our sin and the gospel.

First Corinthians 12:3 states that, without the Spirit, we cannot
confess Jesus. Therefore, the Spirit's aid is needed to repent. He must
act upon us and make our state recognizable to us (John 16:8–11),
remove our demonic glasses (2 Cor. 4:3–4), and give us the grace to
see the glory of God in Jesus Christ (2 Cor. 3:18).

This leads us to another important question: What does the
repentance look like? In short, it is *confession, turning,* and *faith.*

Confession

Confession is the communication of one's individual rebellion
against God, without blame shifting. This looks like one owning
the full extent of one's sin. To illustrate, David exemplifies this well

in Psalm 51:3, "I know my transgressions." The Hebrew word for "know" here is a term of intimacy. David says "my," not "me and Bathsheba." He speaks to God in confession about his own sin and not anyone else's. The psalmist was intimately knowledgeable of his sin. He wasn't blind to the reality of his sin.

You and I cannot repent unless we are generally and specifically clear on the sinfulness of our sin. Generally, we know that we are sinners because the Bible says so. But a general knowledge of sin is not confession; even some unbelievers know they are sinners generally, but would never admit to specific sins they have committed against God and others.

David was clear about the specific rebellion of his own heart—namely falling with Bathsheba. The repentant must understand the collateral damage their sin caused those around them. The repentant don't justify their sin by blaming their environment or the effect of someone else's sin on them, but only acknowledge the sin they committed. Now we can quote 1 John 1:9 with a better spiritual aptitude: "If we confess our sins, he is faithful and just to forgive us our sins and to cleanse us from all unrighteousness." The type of confession that John is speaking of is what we saw in David's song.

One of the most powerful passages on confession's role in repentance is Proverbs 28:13, "Whoever conceals his transgressions will not prosper, but he who confesses and forsakes them will obtain mercy." The word *conceals* is the opposite of confession. This means refusing to acknowledge sin in confession, or perhaps rationalizing away sin. But there is also the one who both "confesses" (הֹדֶם, *modeh*) and "forsakes" (עֹזֵב, *'ozev*) the sin. "To 'confess' sin means to acknowledge sin, to say the same thing about sin that God does."[26]

Our hearts must go along with our confessions. The hypo-
crite confesses his sin but still loves it, like a thief who confesses to stolen goods, yet loves stealing. How many confess
pride and covetousness with their lips but roll them like
honey under their tongue. Augustine said that before his
conversion he confessed sin and begged for power against
it; but his heart whispered within him, "not yet, Lord." He
was afraid to leave his sin too soon. A good Christian is
more honest. His heart keeps pace with his tongue. He is
convinced of the sins that he confesses, and he abhors the
sins that he is convinced of.[27]

My sin is ever before me. About a year had passed between
David's sin of adultery and the time when he acknowledged his
guilt. We know this because Bathsheba had given birth to the child
they conceived together when David confessed his sin (cf. 2 Sam.
12:13–18). David's sin had been on his mind for many months.
Evidently, he had hardened his heart and refused to admit that what
he had done was sinful. Probably, he had rationalized it.[28] But, over
time, David was convicted of his sin and saw his sin the way God
sees it—as sin. David saw that sin, and the implications of sinful
decisions, don't go away. God, by the Spirit, gracefully haunts us
until we repent. True confession comes from this place.

In our growth in Jesus, confession is one of the tools of
restoration. It is a powerful grace from God to know, not that we are
generally fallen, but that our specific sin is sin. We cannot be both
holy and sinful. As we confess our sin to God it is an act of faith,
and we are assured forgiveness and His promise to conform us to
the holy image of Christ.

Turning from Sin

Confession is the first stage of repentance, but turning from our sin is the next. The penitent will find mercy. This expression is a metonymy of cause for the effect—although "mercy" is mentioned, what mercy provides is intended, i.e., forgiveness. In other passages the verb *conceal* is used of God's forgiveness—He covers over the iniquity (Ps. 32:1). "Whoever acknowledges sin, God will cover it; whoever covers it, God will lay it open."[29] This verse is unique in the book of Proverbs; it captures the theology of forgiveness (e.g., Pss. 32 and 51). Every part of the passage is essential to the point: "Confession of sins as opposed to concealing them, coupled with a turning away from them, results in mercy."[30] Abandoning the sin that was committed will result in mercy. Christ frees us by faith to recklessly abandon our sin. We have already escaped through Jesus the corruption that is in the world through sinful desires (2 Pet. 1:4).

When God makes known to us our sin, and we choose to walk in it continuously, we cannot grow intimacy. Our growth is stunted. But for the believer, there is assurance of hope for continued relationship. Only by confession, then turning away, abandoning our sin, can we unleash the power of sanctification in our lives.

Jonah's inauthentic repentance ended in God showing him the consequences of stagnancy in key areas of his life. Even through his embittered disobedience, God used him. God's grace can flow through us in spite of our sin, but repentance unclogs it from flowing to us directly as recipients. Jonah would eventually repent, but wouldn't his life have been different if he obeyed God's commands from the start?

In Psalm 51, one of the first things for which David asked was mercy. Mercy includes not getting what one deserves and forgiveness. In this sense, forgiveness is the removal of guilt and points to the offender having all charges against them dropped, as well as the removal of what caused the guilt in the first place. David knew that if God granted mercy, that meant forgiveness and cleansing.

Repentance is not a one-time event. We never graduate from our need for true repentance. Repentance is a continuing part of our journey with God, not just a part of the start. Owning sin is what makes us Christian.

First, we were oblivious to our sinfulness—both generally and specifically—but made well aware of it by power of the Spirit. We confessed our sin and saw it the way that God sees it. We don't revel in our muck, but commit ourselves, by faith, to the object of our faith: God through Jesus, by the power of the Spirit. As we will see in the chapter on prayer, God frees us to come to Him in our times of brokenness and sinfulness to find favor and mercy, not rejection. We confess our sins before others, and to Him directly. David, upon being confronted with his sin, said, "I have sinned against the LORD" (2 Sam. 12:13). Those six words embodied Proverbs 28:13. Upon his confession and repentance, the Lord said to him, "The LORD also has put away your sin; you shall not die" (2 Sam. 12:13). Mercy! Our walk with Jesus is filled with this as we repent of the sins we will commit. Second, after confession, we abandon our sin by turning away from it. We walk the other way with the help of the Holy Spirit. Yet there is divine empowerment to walk beyond the realm of our sin and that's called *faith*.

What Is Faith?

One of the values that I have seen that can break up male friendships is loyalty. Loyalty is the relational emulsifier of friendships with men. There is an unspoken rule with men (generally speaking), that if I'm wrong, tell me alone, don't agree with others who aren't in our crew publicly. Loyalty is the fraternal bond of human masculinity. For men, the stronger the loyalty, the deeper the friendship.

Faith connects us to the gospel. Faith is the emulsifier that God uses to keep us connected to the gospel. It is what initially connects us to the Jesus. Because of God's grace, and the power of the Spirit willing us, we believe that God guards our salvation in Jesus in eternity (1 Pet. 1:5). Faith keeps us connected to Jesus.

We don't guard our salvation, but God is guarding it. What a powerful reality! Let's be clear: our faith doesn't protect our relationship with God, but God does. Because He is the initiator of our relationship, He keeps us. However, we trust by faith that He is protecting the whole of our salvation. With that level of security we are freed to use our faith to engage in gospel growth.

A great deal of the Hall of Faith (Heb. 11) is about the faith journey of the patriarchs after initial contact with God. The late A. Lewis Patterson had a classic way of describing the patriarchs' faith journeys with God,

Abel worshiped by faith
Enoch walked by faith
Noah worked by faith
Abraham went by faith
David warred by faith

"By faith" is a phrase that shows *how* their faith worked. Faith motivated the works of our spiritual forefathers. Just as faith motivated our forefathers, so must all of our works be rooted in God as the object of our faith. The writer of Hebrews highlighted how faith was the constant motivator on the journey of their fathers, not works of the law. The point is, that a faith walk with God isn't anything new. It is *both* ancient and contemporary. Two verses in the chapter are key to understanding how God uses faith in the life of the believer (11:1, 3). Note that all of the means of grace that are used to grow us is done *by faith*. *By faith* points to the fact that one is dependent on God for what is done in faith.

The Anatomy of Faith

What is faith, exactly? The writer of Hebrews says, "Faith is the assurance of things hoped for, the conviction of things not seen" (11:1). *Assurance* is a powerful term. In one form, it carries meaning that relates to a legal document that declares that an official transferal of a property has taken place. Our assurance in the Lord is rooted in God's guaranteeing something to us in His Word. Assurance tells us we are not alone. The Lord Himself provides assurance on which we can lean.

Hope is the expectation of what God promises. In my estimation, hope is the visionary picture of something God promises that has yet to be, but must be kept before us. Hope is one of the pillars of Christianity because there is still so much to be delivered that has been promised (1 Cor. 13). For our sanctification, it is necessary for our hope to be expanded. The more expansive our hope, the deeper our faith will be.

The Christian faith is filled with so many challenges that hope is a necessary part of what keeps us looking beyond where we are right now. The Hall of Faith points us to the fact that, though many of them didn't receive what they hoped for in their lifetime, their lives were enriched by hoping. They were rewarded for not being fully rewarded.

Paul picks up on this fact in 2 Corinthians—that in the midst of sanctification, what is hoped for is what we can't lose because it is key to our growth (2 Cor. 4:7). We can be perplexed, but not despairing. (Despair is the loss of hope; if we lose hope, then we stop pursuing holiness.)

Conviction is the process that God uses to settle in us that what we are to trust Him for has validity, yet it is unseen. Conviction drives us to move toward the promises of the living God. Faith, then, is rightly said to be the substance of things which are as yet the objects of hope and the evidence of things not seen.[31] God Himself provides verification during our journey with Him. God uses our contact with these points of eternal contact to strengthen us in faith.

God then gives Paul a righteous indignation toward those who were bewitching the Galatians (Gal. 3:1). Someone is trying to convince them to be perfected by human effort, not the work of the Spirit by faith. *Bewitched* is a strong term! "The verb (*baskainō*) can be understood literally here in the sense of bewitching by black magic, but could also be understood figuratively to refer to an act of deception."[32] Removing faith from the equation of our spiritual growth in Jesus is anti-Christian in the strongest sense of the term. You can't get any farther from the Christian faith than witchcraft. It's pound cake without a pound of butter. Whenever we attempt to grow ourselves on our own or think that an activity we do grows us without absolute dependence on the Lord, we are performing witchcraft of sorts.

Faith is meant to be an encouragement in our walk that God is a trustworthy superintendent over our souls. We should be motivated by the assurance of God who promises to do what He said he would do. It is the motivation to pursue holiness by faith. Our Lord encourages us to not faint in faith (Luke 18:1–8). The Lord wants us to be a people marked by faith. Jesus constantly rebukes people about their lack of faith. When the Lord returns I pray that He would find abundant faith in the earth among His chosen people.

Romans 14:23b states, "For whatever does not proceed from faith is sin." Another strong statement about faith. What Paul labels "sin" is any act that does not match our sincerely held convictions about what our Christian faith allows us to do and prohibits us from doing.[33] The immediate context is about Christian liberties. It is clear though that this statement transcends this passage.

We must grow in living our faith before God in clear conviction. As we get into other aspects of what God uses to grow us, faith will permeate every single chapter. We must pray by faith, have faith in God's Word, trust the Holy Spirit to guide us by faith, by faith face our strongholds, and believe God to grow us in our marriage by faith. Everything that the Lord uses to grow us demands trusting in God, not us, and that God would use that means to grow us.

As we seek all God's means of grace, we must see them as just that—mechanisms (means) not mediators (ends). Jesus is our mediator. God lavishes us with His resources to aid our journey in pursuing holiness, in our being conformed to the image of the Lord Jesus Christ. By faith and through repentance, God unleashes His power in our lives.

CHAPTER 4

Grown by the Word of God

love to watch *Chopped*. It is a show on the Food Network where world-class chefs are given mystery ingredients in a contest to prepare a three-course meal. Many times the ingredients are exotic items that aren't easily mixed into the same dish. Chefs are judged on their ability to highlight the ingredients in a meal that possess great presentation, taste, and creativity. Most episodes have at least one chef who forgets to add the key ingredient, or fails to properly feature the key ingredient—making it more of a footnote in the dish. These chefs usually lose the competition.

The Word of God is an essential ingredient to our sanctification and growth. It is impossible to grow without the Word of God. I would call the Word of God a gateway to the means of grace. What I mean by *gateway* is that all of the ways we grow are contained in it. We would not know God, Jesus, the gospel, or any means necessary for growth without the Word of God.

In this chapter we will delve into the role of the Word of God in unleashing the sanctifying work of the Spirit. It will contain the basic ways in which the Word of God calls us to interact practically with God's Word. I love the way Don Whitney puts it:

> True success is promised to those who meditate on God's Word, who think deeply on Scripture, not just at one time each day, but at moments through the day and night. They meditate so much that Scripture saturates their conversation.[34]

We will establish the sufficiency of the Word of God in 2 Timothy 2:15; 3:15–17; and 2 Peter 1:19–21 as the foundation for our relying on the Bible as source of everything necessary for our growth. For most of the chapter, we will explore our role in internalizing, meditating on, and applying the Word to our lives. Again it will be rooted in the Spirit leading us into the truth that is in the Word of God as well as how the gospel empowers us to receive the Word of God.

God-Breathed

I don't care what anyone says, God's Word being breathed out is a magnificent truth. Although God recorded His Word through human authors, He is the one who initiated it, thereby making the Bible His Word. To put it succinctly: God is the divine author of the Bible.

Unlike human beings, who can utter thousands upon thousands of words to no effect, when God speaks, things happen. The connection between the Word of God and creation is not the only exhibition of God's power. Rather, that by which God brought the universe into existence is the same means by which He saves people from sin and death.[35] The same breath that breathed life into

Adam's lungs is the same breath that utters the words of life in the Sermon on the Mount. Amazing, humbling, and mind-blowing.

First Timothy 3:16–17 makes it plain that the Word of God has comprehensive value for the development of God's people throughout the ages. These verses are sandwiched in between two progressive fallen realities. As the age matures into a greater place of wickedness, and people who attend churches are in the midst of the decline, God's people must find their solace in God's Word to grow us in the righteousness of Christ. Second Timothy 3:9 shows that the times are going to get progressively worse. One of the reasons will be an adherence to absolute truth will be tossed asunder, leaving those who deny it in the same place. Paul exhorts Timothy to preach through the various seasons that are mentioned in the former passage (4:1–8). He tells Timothy that even within the ranks of the church, people within the sound of his voice and others who choose to be unwavering heralds of the Word of God will be influenced by the sway of the world. Churches will empty because those who call themselves Christians will leave the faith because *truth* doesn't match what they *feel*. Timothy is told to be sober-minded, to endure suffering, to evangelize lost people, and be faithful to his ministry.

In the midst of this is the sanctifying work of the Word in the lives of the true people of God who seek the Word as God's means to grow them comprehensively. "All Scripture is breathed out by God and profitable for teaching, for reproof, for correction, and for training in righteousness, that the man of God may be complete, equipped for every good work" (2 Tim. 3:16–17). *All Scripture* means every book, every paragraph, and every verse in the revealed Word of God. The more I do expositional preaching through particular books of the Bible, the more I recognize that God doesn't waste His breath. From the popular books and verses, to the so-called minor and obscure, all of God's Word matters for our conformity to the image of Jesus Christ.

The Word of God in this passage (1 Tim. 3:16–17) has four uses and two results. *Teaching* is exposing what God has said so that God's people may understand. *Reproof* is expression of strong disapproval, reproach, and rebuke. *Correction* is the act of offering an improvement (according to a standard) to fix a mistake. *Training in righteousness* is the investment of using God's Word to describe being led from spiritual infancy to spiritual maturity.

Jesus Prayed for This

When I was in college, I went to a historic Baptist church. A lot of who I am in my faith is rooted in the things that the pastors, deacons, and body sowed into my soul during this time. I can remember being in Bible studies that ended in prayer. One of the deacons would pray and it would seem like thunder hit the room. We witnessed the fruit of their prayers, and their relationship with the Lord proved they could "get one through."

Jesus prayed, "Sanctify them in the truth; your word is truth" (John 17:17). That is a powerful prayer request from the Savior. His prayer for us to be sanctified in the truth is for us to be transformed in every sense of the word. It could be that the Lord was praying specifically for the disciples who would launch the global church, but it is likely that this prayer bleeds over to cover all disciples of all time.

The Greek word translated *set . . . apart* is used here in its normal sense of being dedicated, consecrated, or set apart.

The sphere in which the disciples are to be set apart is *in the truth*. In 3:21 the idea of "practicing" (Gk. *doing*) the truth was introduced; in 8:32 Jesus told some of his hearers that if they continued in his word they would truly be his disciples, and would know the truth, and the truth would make them free. These disciples who are with Jesus now for the Farewell Discourse have continued in his word (except for Judas Iscariot, who has departed), and they do know the truth about Jesus and why he has come into the world (17:8). Thus, Jesus can ask the Father to set them apart in this truth as he himself is set apart, so that they might carry on his mission in the world after his departure (note the following verse).[36]

This prayer would be answered in the lives of disciples for millennia. We are now the recipients of this powerful prayer. Jesus prays that our lives would be saturated with the truth. This means all aspects of truth—information, internalization, transformation, and application. Because this is the will of God, we can dive into the Word of God with gospel confidence that the Spirit is working the Word into our hearts and minds for God's desired ends. Jesus continues in John 17:19, "And for their sake I consecrate myself, that they also may be sanctified in truth." The New Living Translation translates the idea more clearly: "And I give myself as a holy sacrifice for them so they can be made holy by your truth." So the death of Christ is the means by which the truth is released to us to dedicate us and sanctify us for the living God. Without the gospel, there will be no transformation. Daily faith in the gospel, as we are exposed by various means to the Word of God, is what gives us access for connection.

I have been given an iTunes gift card on several occasions. The resources are uploaded to my account. However, I am not given access to what I want until I log in. I cannot download any music, movies, or television shows unless I log in and gain access. Faith is the login for our access to the Word of God, through the gospel. Reading, meditation, memorization, preaching, hearing, etc.—we must pursue all of these outlets to be exposed to God's Word. We will explore later in the chapter sections of which are made available for us to be sanctified in the truth.

The issue is that we have to trust that what God says is true. That is why the psalmist says, "The sum of your word is truth" (Ps. 119:160). In order to receive something, we must believe that it is true or trust it. We must trust God by trusting in all that He says. Our greatest obstacle to growth is trusting that the heart of God is telling the truth. It is one thing to "Amen" what is in the Word with our lips, but in our hearts deny it. Consequently, the growth point for us must be, "For all the promises of God find their Yes in him. That is why it is through him that we utter our Amen to God for his glory" (2 Cor. 1:20). Our growth depends on the Holy Spirit applying to our souls what's implanted. *Implanted* means marked by being deeply fixed or set within something. To put it differently, implanted is permanently established in the individual and, like inborn assets, functions in an exceptional manner.[37] Meaning, having the Word in us so deeply that it is as if the Word is a part of our soul's nature. It is at the core of being born again.

The Law Helps Us to See

Criminals are dangerous because they disregard the law. Laws (for the most part) are put in place to establish order in society. Without laws, there is anarchy and the potential for licentiousness. Law exists in the natural sphere because sin does (and sin establishes disorder). The presence of law assumes the sinfulness of man. If man were governed by God's character, there would be no need for law.

Just as human laws point out the sinfulness of man, so also does divine law. We cannot understand the Word of God without understanding the role of the law established in the OT and the fulfillment of the law in Christ in the NT. The law exposes sin, which, as we have already said, stunts our spiritual growth. We cannot grow in sanctification if we are lawless people. Paul says, "What then shall we say? That the law is sin? By no means! Yet if it had not been for the law, I would not have known sin" (Rom. 7:7). While showing man to be sinful, the law shows off the holiness of the living God. Are we under the law? No, but it is still profitable for doctrine (2 Tim. 3:16). We can't appreciate Jesus Christ if we don't appreciate what He came to fulfill. So to appreciate the law is to revere Jesus. The law makes us see our need for mercy and transformation through the gospel. As we see our need for mercy it drives us to the gospel. In Christ the law instructs us in righteousness under the New Covenant.

That is why Paul says,

Now we know that the law is good, if one uses it lawfully, understanding this, that the law is not laid down for the just but for the lawless and disobedient, for the ungodly and sinners, for the unholy and profane, for those who strike their fathers and mothers, for murderers, the sexually immoral, men who practice homosexuality, enslavers, liars, perjurers, and whatever else is contrary to sound doctrine, in accordance with the gospel of the glory of the blessed God with which I have been entrusted. (1 Tim. 1:8–11)

In other words, the law helps us all *to see*. We cannot confess our sin, unless we clearly see our sin. So we cannot be sanctified according to God's plan, unless we are understanding sin according to the law in the Word of God.

Means of Biblical Renewal

All of us as humans think, act, value, and have affections that are all shaped by how we filter everything we experience. Some would call this a worldview. I define worldview as, "a grid through which these followers of Jesus Christ view, interact with, and understand God, people, and the world."[38] One of the most important things to understand is that mind renewal doesn't happen by osmosis, rather by intentional interaction with the Word of God. The Holy Spirit applies God's Word to us, but we have to do the hard work of being in places where the Word is dispensed. To be doers of the Word, we must be hearers of the Word.

Romans 12:1–2 and Ephesians 4:23 call us to renew our minds. Mind renewal is at the core of sanctification. If change happens in our minds, it will happen in every other part of the body. *Mind* and *heart*, when it comes to sanctification in the Bible, are the same thing. Both point to *the core of who we are*. In our hearts and minds lay our hopes, dreams, and beliefs. If we aren't changed on that level, our lives remain captive to our natural way of thinking and are deeply vulnerable to the Devil. God's truth sets us free.

When we say *means*, we mean *God-ordained access points* that Jesus has given to those who believe. Through His sacrificial death, He has given us access to make the most of our lives. As the key of David, He unlocks the things of God. He unleashes the power of the Spirit embedded in His Word.

There is a difference between what we *have* to do and what we *want* to do. I delight in shopping for clothes and eating at great restaurants (when I can afford to). I delight in sunny days with beautiful weather. I delight in my family. In essence, all of us can make a grand list of what we delight. *Delight*, at its core, means to have intense pleasure and satisfaction in someone, something, or someplace.

The psalmist states that the people that experience the greatest amount of sustainable joy and happiness are those who have intense pleasure and satisfaction with the Word of God. In other words, when one is delighting in God's Word, it causes the blessedness of verse one to enter into every area of human experience. For instance, a gentleman I know is on a certain diet and does a particular type of workout. No matter where he is, somehow, the conversation moves towards the topic of diet and workouts. Once he gets started, it is almost impossible to curb the subject. He has an insatiable delight for health and fitness. He doesn't *have* to exercise; he *wants* to.

In comparison, that is how our passion for the Word of God must be. Now that isn't to say that we should be browbeating people with the Scriptures; however, we must have a preoccupation with and a desire for the Word of God to a great enjoyment.

Meditate on the Word: Delight in Psalms looks like meditation that flows from memorization. Anything that we delight in, we store the knowledge of it within us. In order to delight in the Word, we must have a continued relationship with it; we must store knowledge of the Word in our hearts.

To truly delight in the Word is to delight oneself in the Lord. Spurgeon says,

> He is not *under* the law as a curse and condemnation, but he is *in* it, and he delights to be in it as his rule of life; he delights, moreover, to *meditate* in it, to read it *by day,* and think upon it *by night.* He takes a text and carries it with him all day long; and in the night-watches, when sleep forsakes his eyelids, he museth upon the Word of God. In the *day* of his prosperity he sings *psalms* out of the Word of God, and in the *night* of his affliction he comforts himself with *promises* out of the same book. "The law of the Lord" is the daily bread of the true believer. And yet, in David's day, how small was the volume of inspiration, for they had scarcely anything save the first five books of Moses! How much more, then, should we prize the whole written Word which it is our privilege to have in all our houses! But, alas, what ill-treatment is given to this angel from heaven! We are not all Berean searchers of the Scriptures. How few among us can lay claim to the benediction of the text! Perhaps some of you can claim a sort of negative purity, because you do not walk in the way of the ungodly; but let me ask you—Is your delight in the law of God? Do you study God's Word? Do you make it the man of your right

hand—your best companion and hourly guide? If not, this blessing belongeth not to you.[39]

In Deuteronomy 6:4–9, it is clear that our love and delight for the Lord should be rooted in a preoccupation with His Word. Every sector of our lives must be informed by the Word of God. My desire isn't just to have a devotional time with the Lord, but a devotional lifestyle. We must not spend a moment in the day with God, but all of our day must be lived in light of the divine presence. Delight is nurtured by soaking all day in the Word. To delight in God's Word is to delight in sanctification. That type of exposure to the Word always leads to intense growth in the Lord.

One of my closest friends, Blake Wilson, embodies this—and it's convicting. He has such a delight in the Word it is known by all. If he finds a treasure, he wants to share it with all his friends and family. I remember when books were less portable than they are now, he would have a backpack filled with three to four translations of the Bible. He would highlight up all those Bibles. Blake would, many times, create his own verse chain in the margins of those Bibles. If there was a topic or verse that hermeneutically related to other passages, he would write the references in the margin of each page. When you looked at his Bibles, they bled like one who *delights*. You could ask him where almost any verse is in the Bible and he could tell you.

What is beautiful about his love for God's Word isn't showboating. He loves the good Lord and His Word. As you spend time with him, you cannot help but desire what he has with the Lord.

Our spiritual life should be filled with moments of red-hot pursuit of the Lord. At the core of having healthy and powerful

spiritual life is found a delight for the Word of God. Jonathan
Edwards was that sort of Christian:

> That religion which God requires, and will accept, does
> not consist in weak, dull, and lifeless wishes, raising us
> but a little above a state of indifference: God, in his word,
> greatly insists upon it, that we be good in earnest, "fervent
> in spirit," and our hearts vigorously engaged in religion:
> Rom. 12:11, "Be ye fervent in spirit, serving the Lord."
> Deut. 10:12, "And now, Israel, what doth the Lord thy God
> require of thee, but to fear the Lord the God, to walk in all
> his ways, and to love him, and to serve the Lord thy God
> with all thy heart, and with all thy soul?" and chap. 6:4–6,
> "Hear, O Israel, the Lord our God is one Lord: And thou
> shalt love the Lord thy God with all thy heart, and with all
> thy might." It is such a fervent vigorous engagedness of the
> heart in religion, that is the fruit of a real circumcision of
> the heart, or true regeneration, and that has the promises
> of life; Deut. 30:6, "And the Lord thy God will circumcise
> thine heart, and the heart of thy seed, to love the Lord thy
> God with all thy heart, and with all thy soul, that thou
> mayest live."[40]

As many have said on this subject, the church has let Eastern
religions hijack one of the most powerful means of grace for spiritual
growth. Meditation for the Christian isn't clearing or emptying our
minds, but it is to fill our minds with God's Word. Meditation is
what develops us in the quality of how we absorb the Word.

Christian meditation involves filling your mind with God and His truth. For some, meditation is an attempt to achieve complete mental passivity, but biblical meditation requires constructive mental activity. Worldly meditation employs visualization techniques intended to "create your own reality." And while Christian history has always had a place for the sanctified use of our God-given imagination in meditation, imagination is our servant to help us meditate on things that are true (see Philippians 4:8). Furthermore, instead of "creating our own reality" through visualization, we link meditation with prayer to God and responsible, Spirit-filled human action to effect changes. . . . In addition to these distinctives, let's define meditation as deep thinking on the truths and spiritual realities revealed in Scripture, or upon life from a scriptural perspective, for the purposes of understanding, application, and prayer. Meditation goes beyond hearing, reading, studying, and even memorizing as a means of taking in God's Word. . . . Reading, studying, and memorizing God's Word are like additional plunges of the tea bag into the cup. The more frequently the tea enters the water, the more permeating its effect. Meditation, however, is like immersing the bag completely and letting it steep until all the rich tea flavor has been extracted and the hot water is thoroughly tinctured reddish brown. Meditation on Scripture is letting the Bible brew in the brain.[41]

Letting the Word richly dwell in us (Col. 3:16) is done through meditation. Our meditation doesn't make improvements upon the Word, but it is about the intensity of our absorption of it. As our minds are plunged into the Word through constant repetitious mediation, we find ourselves saturated. As we muse on, consider, think on, ponder and so give serious consideration to information, or a situation[42] we find ourselves at the center of taking the Word very seriously. To let the Word dwell richly within us is for the density of the Word to be realized. There is a chocolate cake at The Cheesecake Factory that has layers and layers of chocolate. It is so rich you have to eat it in stages. As a matter of fact, it took me a week to finish it and, to be honest, I didn't quite finish it. When the Word of God is meditated on, it is digested in stages. Slow, thoughtful pondering is what meditating on the Word of God entails.

Hear the Word (Rom. 10:17): Truly hearing the Word is one of the main entryways for being sanctified by the Word of God. Because our hearts are changed by the gospel, believers in Jesus are good soil (Ezek. 36:25–27). Obviously we can disobey the Word or have strongholds that impede us from receptivity. However, by nature, we are empowered to have a receptive heart. Therefore, truly hearing the Word does not mean the Word passing through our auditory senses but coming into our hearts by faith.

Hearing the Word requires we put ourselves in the path of those who are speaking the Word. It means you don't forsake gathering together for the preaching of the Word (Heb. 10:25); it means you load up your iPhone with sermons that expose the Word; it means you stand shoulder to shoulder with the men at the mission who sit under the preaching of a gospel evangelist; it means that anywhere the gospel is preached, you discipline yourself to aim your path to intersect so that you can hear the Word.

Merely hearing the Word is not the point. Hearing the Word is *always* for the purpose of *doing* the will of God, as we will see.

Receive the Word (James 1:21): Whereas, hearing the Word is about exposure to the Word, receiving the Word is about internalizing what is heard. It is one thing to hear God's Word, but it is another thing to receive what is being said by faith. James places hearing and receiving in the same context to make this idea so clear to us:

> Therefore put away all filthiness and rampant wickedness and *receive* with meekness the implanted word, which is able to save your souls. But be doers of the word, and not hearers only, deceiving yourselves. For if anyone is a *hearer* of the word and not a doer, he is like a man who looks intently at his natural face in a mirror. (James 1:21–23, emphasis added)

In other words, we can be a hearer, but not a receiver. But we cannot be a receiver and not a hearer. Yet more broadly, true hearing is receiving, leading to doing.

What the great gospel did was set our radios to heaven's frequency. The key phrase is, "able to save your souls." How can a saved person be *more* saved, if they are saved? Well, the word for *saved* here—as we saw in the first chapter—can refer to *getting saved* (justification), *being saved* (sanctification), or *will be saved in the end* (glorification). We must recognize that the implanted Word of God is necessary for the Spirit to use it to grow us in every step of salvation. This is how we participate in His plan to grow us—we not only hear the Word, but receive the Word.

Study the Word (2 Tim. 2:15): In my city, there are three religions that are dominant: Islam, Jehovah's Witnesses, and Catholicism. Of the three, Islam and Jehovah's Witnesses seem to have the best understanding of what they believe and how belief should connect to faithful practice. As a pastor, I come into contact with many Christians who are connected to the practical implications of faith, rather than the Christian faith itself (which could be a conversion issue). It frustrates me to meet Muslims and Jehovah's Witnesses in Philly who demonstrate more faithful study of their faith and how their faith applies to their lives than many in my neighborhood who profess to be Christians.

As a pastor, I am sensitive to the pressing, practical needs in a congregation. Sermons, and every area of pastoral ministry, ought to be aimed at meeting those needs. I am always pondering, in my prep, my responsibility, by the power of the Spirit, to connect the Scriptures to real life. However, I find that the average Christian is bored and closed off to learning what is necessary for faith. It's what makes faith, faith. Many of us are more concerned about God meeting our needs than knowing and loving Him. So we shirk the responsibility to study.

As important as "devotional insights" are, we need the rich nutrients of the Word within us to grow. That gospel growth is the means He uses to answer our prayers, meet our needs, and fix our problems. Believers need to study the Word and grow in knowledge of the heart and mind of Christ.

Studying God's Word isn't just for the pastor, or for seasoned saints, but for every believer. Every Christian is held in place by God through the truth that has made us free. Paul tells Timothy to, "Do your best to present yourself to God as one approved, a worker who has no need to be ashamed, rightly handling the word of truth" (2 Tim. 2:15).

"Present yourself approved," or like the old King James Version, "study to shew *thyself* approved." For Timothy, as the lead communicator of God's Word in Ephesus, this would be applied immediately for pastoral leadership. However, I suspect that on some level, this should have a subapplication for all believers. These letters were circulated and read aloud by churches. Other believers would receive the same instruction as Timothy. The point of the verse is the presentation of one's self to God, which is the only way to communicate God's Word with accuracy. With this in mind, shouldn't we all—on some level, as believers—be built up with accurate understanding of God's Word that comes from careful study?

To take it one step further, in Hebrews 5:11–6:2, the writer assumes that the body should be a community of disciple-makers. Because they have waned in their spiritual growth by growing in God's means of grace, they needed to be reeducated in the elementary things about Jesus Christ. These elementary teachings about Jesus were the fundamental truths that were taught at the beginning stages of first-century Christians' sanctification. Without them, growth would be stunted.

Here is the list: "Therefore let us leave the elementary doctrine of Christ and go on to maturity, not laying again a foundation of repentance from dead works and of faith toward God, and of instruction about washings, the laying on of hands, the resurrection of the dead, and eternal judgment" (Heb. 6:1–2). Basically, the writer says they need to be retaught basic Christian doctrine: repentance and faith in Christ alone for salvation, baptism, the Lord's Supper, church government, and the return of Jesus Christ. They need to be taught the Word. All of the items entailed under these were areas that were taught as a standard to new believers and were helpful

for spiritual growth. All of the teachings mentioned here are called
milk level (Heb. 5:12–13).

Many of you reading might consider these items as beyond your
level of comprehension, but here they are only the beginning. The
average Christian, if they were asked to briefly explain these, might
feel as if they were in an ordination process. But these are *elementary*
teachings. We must know them to walk by faith and we must walk
by faith in the faith to grow. And to *know* we must *study*.

Understand this: *knowing* is not merely about facts or information. It is about having a clear understanding of what we believe so
that we can exercise faith and grow. As we grow in our knowledge
of God, it will impact our experiences with God. We cannot *love
God* without *knowing God*—and vice versa.

Christians, like everyone else, find that they go through very
difficult things in life. And if they process those experiences devoid
of an understanding of God, it can make an already difficult
situation worse. In our church, we had a young adult who lost a close
family member in a tragic accident. When it happened, my wife
and I found ourselves in the trenches helping this person through
this crisis. Many of the questions that arose during this time felt
like we were defending God in a trial. God and His heart were
being questioned in light of new evidence. This tragedy exposed
the shallow spiritual roots in the life of this hurting parishioner.
Though it was hard, it was an opportunity to strengthen their faith
through knowing God more deeply. The more I pastor people
through hardships, the more I am convinced that people need deep
roots in the truth of God's Word.

To unleash the power of the Spirit of God to conform us to the
image of Christ, we have to unleash the Word of God in our lives.

We must meditate on the Word, hear the Word, receive the Word, and study and know the Word. The Word of God breathes new life into our lungs—the same breath that God breathed into Adam.

A popular quote attributed to Spurgeon goes like this, "The Word of God is like a lion. You don't have to defend a lion. All you have to do is let the lion loose, and the lion will defend itself." Unleash the Word of God in your life; you'll never be the same.

CHAPTER 5

Prayer

As easy as prayer may seem, it can become the most difficult spiritual discipline in our lives. We see celebrities pray at award shows, athletes pray when they achieve their goals, and fictional characters pray in movies when their situation seems beyond their own power. And prayer is often the first step of faith for a new believer—the first thing that occurs to us to do when we believe and are transformed by the gospel.

Prayer seems easy, because it is. But to have the sort of prayer life that unleashes the sanctifying power of the Spirit in our lives requires more than the ritual of displaying the sign of the cross in the end zone after a touchdown. It requires—just like every other aspect of sanctification—God's help.

Simply put, prayer is having a conversation with God. We have all the access to the living God through Jesus Christ through prayer. Leonard Ravenhill put it the best, "Prayer is profoundly simple and simply profound. 'Prayer is the simplest form of speech that infant lips can try,' and yet so sublime that it outranges all speech and exhausts man's vocabulary."[43] Jesus died to open heaven to us. An open heaven!

Prayer is everywhere in the NT, and for good reason. Almost every book of the NT has prayer contained therein, or at least some sort of reference to prayer. In the larger books like Romans and Luke, to smaller ones like Philemon and Jude, prayer is there. Obviously, in God's revelation to man, He saw it necessary that we should know how to pray.

As you read these prayers, you can begin to see that many of them are about spiritual growth. It is clear that prayer is another core component to our growth in which the Spirit uses through the gospel to grow us.

> Another crucial element of a healthy spiritual diet is regular attention to prayer. Prayer is often one of the neglected elements in a person's spiritual walk. Prayer is the means by which we offer up our desires unto God and is the arena in which we often wrestle with him in the struggle to seek greater sanctification. In prayer we can cry aloud to God and ask him to sanctify us further. Do you lack faith? Plead with God that he would strengthen it. Do you lack hope? Pray to God that he would fill you with it. In prayer, we look to the risen and ascended Messiah who ministers in the heavenly Holy of holies.[44]

We will not grow unless we pray.

What Is Prayer?

Prayer is the chamber in which the sinner-turned-saint builds deeper fellowship with God (Matt. 6:5–15; Heb. 4:14; 10:19–23), aligns with the will of God (Ps. 37:4; Luke 22:42; Heb. 5:7–10), and intercedes on behalf others (Jesus and Pauline prayers).

Prayer is not merely individual in nature, but can be applied to the corporate setting as well. One of the first things the disciples devoted themselves to, after the pouring out of the Spirit in Acts 2, was prayer together. If we relegate prayer to our prayer closets only and not to the church as well, we are missing out on a key aspect of prayer. The Spirit desires to conform the entire body of Christ to the image of Christ through prayer together.

Building *deeper fellowship* involves confession and repentance (1 John 1:9), extoling His majesty (Ps. 104), venting (Ps. 62:8), and just being with Him (Ps. 46:10). The bulk of most of the believer's prayer life is filled with this area. Our lives must be driven by these things being a major part of how we engage in contact with God in prayer. No matter how short or long, we must make prayer part of our daily regimen. Not just at one time in the day, but planned prayer throughout our days.

Being *aligned with the will of God* is what happens by listening to God. When we pray often enough to not only speak to God, but to listen to God, the result will be our will and God's will coming into conflict with one another—you can speculate about who you think is going to win this wrestling match. But many of us don't pray enough to wrestle with our King. We must not be strangers to heaven's throne; God expects to see us regularly at the throne of grace.

One of the most powerful messages that I ever heard was by my "sage," Dr. Crawford Loritts. He said, "We must live in a place of constant state of constant God-neediness." Oh how I long to live such a life! I want, in weakness, for no one to wonder where I will run. I want people to know that I am at the throne, looking for aid in the time of need. In my brokenness, I want to be so predictable that people will assume I am with my Father. A life marked by disciplined prayer conform our wills into the kind of people who say, "Not my will, but Yours be done."

Intercession is the one all of us can stand to benefit from, and need to do more. It is the most sacrificial because it involves growing in empathy toward the needs of others. The barometer of our love for others shines through in how much we are found before the throne, not just for ourselves, but for others. Jesus stated several times how He was praying for the growth of His disciples. As a matter of fact, His major ministry on our behalf at the right hand of God is to make intersession for us. To be conformed to the image of Christ means praying the way He prayed, through the ministry of intercession.

Drawing Near to God

When I received discipline from my parents, it was—to say the very least—extremely difficult. My parents were hardcore disciplinarians. But in many ways, this was helpful for me. By being constantly disciplined, I never wondered about where the boundaries were. Though I continued to behave in ways that warranted strong discipline, I understood what was acceptable and what was not.

On the other hand, I often didn't know when I was restored to fellowship with my parents. My punishments didn't have time limits, I didn't know when I would regain the privileges I lost through discipline. Though the boundaries of transgression were clear, the conditions of restoration were unclear. So as I grew older, I struggled with acceptance in some ways, although I believed that they disciplined me as best they knew how.

One of the major points that the Bible seeks to drive home is the fact that we have access to God through the Lord Jesus Christ. For instance, the book of Hebrews is written to show how superior our access to Christ is compared to prior means of access to God. The theme of *draw near* is a constant refrain in the book. (*Draw near* is recorded nineteen times.) One of the most memorable verses containing the phrase is one you've probably heard before: "Let us then with confidence draw near to the throne of grace, that we may receive mercy and find grace to help in time of need" (Heb. 4:16). Our *drawing near,* most often, is understood as coming to God in prayer.

It is hard for us today—because we are not under the rule of a monarch—to comprehend the depth of this imagery. But it is rich, deep, compelling, humbling! We have to understand the kingdom imagery of the Bible if we are to understand it all. C. E. Arnold helps us gain perspective:

> Monarchs of the ancient world sat on thrones as symbols of their power and authority. Consequently, to approach a monarch's throne could be a fearsome act, for one was at the mercy of the ruler, who had the power of life and death in hand. The throne imagery also carried over into religious beliefs. . . . When used with reference to the gods, a throne also was a symbol of power and authority. In Christian

belief God's throne is a seat of authority and power, but, as Hebrews points out, it too is a seat of grace. Thus, the believer who has Christ as his high priest can approach the throne with "confidence" or boldness. In Hellenistic Judaism and early Christianity the concept of drawing near to God with confidence refers especially to approaching God in prayer.[45]

The call to confidence implies that the coming to the throne of a ruler might not naturally inspire confidence. It might be dangerous to approach the throne. It might be that the king is not willing to grant requests of his subjects. It might be that the king has a habit of humiliating any who approach with a request. But the Lord Jesus communicates through His Word that we should approach the King of all creation with *confidence.*

In essence, confidence is a trait that requires willingness to undertake activities that involve risk. God, in His infinite power, is worthy of fear. He spoke the world into existence; He could just as easily destroy it. As a rebellious creation, we have defied the King, and brought further risk onto ourselves in our rebellion. Why would we ever risk approaching the throne of a king with whom we have declared war as our enemy? Make no mistake, our sin is a war declaration against a sovereign ruler.

Because Jesus has given His life, we have access to the presence of the King by which no one can stand before. Jesus has turned the enemies of God into His loyal subjects. God's wrath, which ought to be exercised on every subject in the kingdom who sought to subvert His rule, has been satisfied by the death of Christ. Since God's wrath has been extinguished, we don't relate to God's throne as ones who are worthy of wrath, but as recipients of grace. Christ stood before the throne on our behalf and withstood all wrath, took all of the risk, so that all is left for those who follow Him in confidence. We now come as court officials, princes, brothers of the King's sons and daughters, inheritors of the kingdom, when we make our requests. We approach with confidence because there is no longer anything to fear!

Consequently, God invites us to His throne, even while we are in sin, to talk to Him. What we find is mercy and grace, not wrath and judgment. Why are we still able to draw near when in our sin? Because of this: "Therefore, brothers, since we have confidence to enter the holy places by the blood of Jesus, by the new and living way that he opened for us through the curtain, that is, through his flesh, and since we have a great priest over the house of God, let us draw near with a true heart in full assurance of faith, with our hearts sprinkled clean from an evil conscience and our bodies washed with pure water" (Heb. 10:19–22). Even when we betray the King, the sin of spiritual high treason, His court remains open to our coming to Him for help.

Prayer for Growth

One of the most peculiar verses in the Bible is about the prayer life of the Lord Jesus Christ in His time on earth. Hebrews 5:7–9 says,

> In the days of his flesh, Jesus offered up prayers and supplications, with loud cries and tears, to him who was able to save him from death, and he was heard because of his reverence. Although he was a son, he learned obedience through what he suffered. And being made perfect, he became the source of eternal salvation to all who obey him.

It is clear that prayer was a huge part of the learning of Jesus. Even though Jesus was born perfect in both His humanity and His divine nature, in His humanity He learned. "Learned obedience," means that in His humanity, He submitted to growth. I won't begin to try to explain this mystery, but between His sufferings and His prayers there were components of His learning in His life on earth. It is striking that throughout the Gospels we see the Lord praying. If the Lord needed to pray, how much more do we, who are being perfected from our old selves, need this? Jesus wasn't being perfected from a sin nature; He was merely maturing in His already perfected perfection.

> According to Hebrews, Jesus, who was without sin (4:15), was obedient throughout his life. On his entry into the world he announced that he delighted to do God's will (10:5–10). "To learn obedience," then, meant coming to appreciate fully what conforming to God's will involved. But this is not to suggest that Jesus had previously been disobedient, and now needed to grasp what it meant to obey the will of God. Rather, authentic obedience is practiced in particular, concrete circumstances. So, as Jesus encountered fresh situations—and the focus of the text is on his suffering—his faithfulness to God was challenged, and his unfailing obedience to the Father's will was tested again and again.[46]

Our growth is rooted in Him, therefore our prayers should be an imitation of Christ.

As stated earlier, much of the NT prayers are prayers for our growth. Obedience doesn't grow us, as much as it is a barometer of our growth. Therefore, Paul, in his doxological prayer in Romans, prays for the gospel to be preached and believers to be strengthened by the Holy Spirit through that preaching, and obedience of faith in the gospel may be a result. Obeying by faith—in others words, He wants faith-based obedience, not law-based, religious, moralistic obedience.

What if all we did flowed from obedient faith in the gospel? What if we allowed the grace of the gospel to motivate every area of our lives? Where would the church of Jesus Christ be if our lives were in such a place? It would be the most powerful way we can live. What is amazing about Paul's prayer is that our lives are on a trajectory of faith-based obedience in the gospel of Jesus Christ. May our lives be such to the glory of the good Lord.

Spurgeon has two chapters on prayer in his classic, *Lectures to My Students*. In the chapter on "The Preacher's Private Prayer," he urges that the prayer life for the preacher should show itself in his life and ministry. Spurgeon argues that an effective preaching ministry flows from a sanctifying life wrought through prayer. In the mind of Spurgeon, to neglect prayer is to neglect accessing God, who has promised spiritual growth for the preacher and his hearers. He writes,

> Of course the preacher is above all others distinguished as a man of prayer. He prays as an ordinary Christian, else he were a hypocrite. He prays more than ordinary Christians, else he were disqualified for the office which he has undertaken. "It would be wholly monstrous," says Bernard, "for a man to be highest in office and lowest in soul; first in station and last in life." Over all his other relationships

the pre-eminence of the pastor's responsibility casts a halo, and if true to his Master, he becomes distinguished for his prayerfulness in them all. As a citizen, his country has the advantage of his intercession; as a neighbor those under his shadow are remembered in supplication. He prays as a husband and as a father; he strives to make his family devotions a model for his flock; and if the fire on the altar of God should burn low anywhere else, it is well tended in the house of the Lord's chosen servant—for he takes care that the morning and evening sacrifice shall sanctify his dwelling.[47]

Not only does the preacher need to find their strength for growth, life, and ministry in prayer, but all God's people.

Praying Versus Complaining

It is easy to complain; it's difficult to faithfully pray. We complain about what we don't have, we complain about our jobs, our children, our spouse or our singleness, the church, our neighbors, our cities. But we don't recognize prayer as the catalyst of change from God.

It grieves me that, in the church, we complain about what's wrong with the church, instead of praying for change by the Spirit. Paul's prayers for the church were mostly for its growth. Before Paul talked crazy to the church, he let her know that he'd been praying for her. You think your church is dysfunctional? Read Paul's letter to the church at Corinth. Paul had plenty to complain about, and though he rebuked the church, he never failed to pray for her. The difference between complaining and godly correction in the equation is prayer. If your church is in need of correction, don't open your mouth to anyone before you cry out to God in prayer.

Leonard Ravenhill states,

> No man is greater than his prayer life. The pastor who is not praying is playing; the people who are not praying are straying. The pulpit can be a shopwindow to display one's talents; the prayer closet allows no showing off. Poverty-stricken as the Church is today in many things, she is most stricken here, in the place of prayer. We have many organizers, but few agonizers; many players and payers, few prayers; many singers, few clingers; lots of pastors, few wrestlers; many fears, few tears; much fashion, little passion; many interferers, few intercessors; many writers, but few fighters. Failing here, we fail everywhere. The two prerequisites to successful Christian living are vision and passion, both of which are born in and maintained by prayer. The ministry of preaching is open to few; the ministry of prayer—the highest ministry of all human offices—is open to all.[48]

It does us no good to try and solve our problems alone. We lack the power to change. We need to assess our lives in prayer for God's transformative power to intervene.

Our prayers must reflect what Christ has accomplished for us. Praying the will of God means to pray the implications of the gospel on issues in our lives that the gospel may inform. This is for our sanctification. Case in point, in 2 Thessalonians, Paul speaks of this, "We ought always to give thanks to God for you, brothers, as is right, because your faith is growing abundantly, and the love of every one of you for one another is increasing. Therefore we ourselves boast about you in the churches of God for your steadfastness and faith in all your persecutions and in the afflictions that you are enduring" (2 Thess. 1:3–4).

God cares about the issues in your life! Your troubles, your challenges, your trials all matter—the gospel has something to say about every one of them. Many times, Paul's thanksgivings are a continued prayer for the people of God. We see that as Paul encourages them, that God is already at work in the midst of their suffering. By speaking of their steadfastness and faith in sufferings and persecution, Paul reminds them of what they already know—God is still with them.

Prayer is not the dictation of our will to God, but our alignment with His will. Prayer is used by God to grow us, because as we spend time in prayer, God melts us and molds us into His Son's image.

As we spend time in the presence of God in prayer, we find ourselves praying what we wouldn't have prayed before. Prayer transports us into heaven's throne room by faith; we find ourselves in His presence. To find ourselves in His presence is not dissimilar to Isaiah's experience—we cannot remain the same. Because we have access to God through Jesus Christ we must take advantage of such a powerful opportunity that is only afforded to the redeemed.

In order to unleash God's sanctifying power in our lives, we must pray in faith, by the power of the Spirit, for the alignment of our will to the will of Christ, in whose image we are being conformed.

CHAPTER 6

The Role of Suffering in Sanctification

G rowing up in D.C. during the late 1970s and early '80s was as fun as it was dangerous. It was fun because in this city we learned to become innovative by creating for ourselves what wasn't otherwise available. We made basketball courts out of plastic milk crates and de-spoked bicycle rims; we used rocks to chalk our court lines, or to play four corners; girls jumped rope using old pieces of wire cords. Everything that might have been readily available to other communities had to be invented with what we had available in ours. We had a lot of fun.

But our context was dangerous too. My house was falling apart and should have been condemned. As time went on, a small rock began appearing on our streets that contained the seeds of their own destruction: crack cocaine. It became a powerful economic and social force in every urban city from L.A. to N.Y., from D.C. to Miami.

The sound of gunshots became the background noise to all the fun we had as kids. Friends were getting killed and incarcerated. I wanted out!

My quest became leaving, never to return to this type of urban environment again. For me, getting out of the inner city was a natural progression of life. It was the hope that life gets better, and reflected the fact that I was on a better path. My goal was to build a life that was impervious to suffering—financial suffering, dangerous neighborhoods, inadequate education, etc. I went to college just to get out, and got hit up with the gospel. I was discipled two years later, called to the ministry, and was in seminary one year later. I figured, at this point, I had achieved my goal—physically removing myself from environments where I could ever suffer. How wrong was I?

It wasn't long before I found out that God would have me at a crossroads with different suffering on life's journey. That's not just true for me, but true for you—a promise for all of God's people.

While at Dallas Theological Seminary, we had to take five semesters of Greek which amounted to two and a half years of study. The final class in that series was called 203. Dr. Lawry's focus for us was to help us to develop an exegetical picture of the book of Romans. Of course, we had to translate it from the original language, which was a beast. However, the capstone of the class was a paper on—you guessed it—sanctification. He instructed us to write a paper on an aspect of sanctification addressed by Paul in the book of Romans. Dr. Lawry told me that my particular paper topic on the subject would have been the first of its type during his tenure. No pressure, right?

As I surveyed the NT and began isolating the verses from Matthew to Revelation, it wasn't long before I realized how massive a theme this was. There are so many practical issues that intersect with sanctification. Alongside issues like money, sex, false teachers, and other subjects, which are huge in the NT, I found that suffering is a major theme.

Jesus, Paul, James, and Peter speak about the expectation of suffering for believers. Acts descriptively speaks of what the former prescribe as a part of the journey for the believer. There is an expectation in the NT that as the believer witnesses to the reign of Christ to a world that does not know Him, persecution will happen. However, one of the telling things in these passages that makes its way to the forefront is the fact that the Lord uses suffering from *without* and *within* as a means to grow us in Him, and conform us to the image of Jesus Christ.

Jesus Sets the Pattern

Suffering is antithetical to who we are because we are driven by self-preservation. We try to preserve ourselves by minimizing danger where we work, where we educate ourselves, and where we live. We see this in the cycles of gentrification in urban centers. Especially as a pastor in urban ministry you see the flip-flop of people between the suburbs and city centers, driven by desire for comfort and survival. Let me say that there is nothing wrong with wanting to be safe, or to pursue the best opportunities for one's family. But for the Christian, our drive must always originate in the gospel, not merely self-preservation. Thus, we must not seek suffering—the Bible never says that—but in our walk with Jesus Christ, we should expect that suffering will happen, and we must not allow it to redirect our mission.

Our Lord, even prior to His incarnation, was set on a path to suffering. Isaiah 53 is a brutal description of the demise of the Messiah. Psalm 22 depicts His death. Zechariah 13:7 speaks of the fact the Good Shepherd would be struck down. In the course of Jesus' ministry we see that He was clearly cognizant of this reality as imminent. Early in His ministry Jesus says, "Let these words sink into your ears: The Son of Man is about to be delivered into the hands of men" (Luke 9:44). Mark quotes Jesus saying, "For he was teaching his disciples, saying to them, 'The Son of Man is going to be delivered into the hands of men, and they will kill him. And when he is killed, after three days he will rise'" (Mark 9:31). Matthew shows later in His ministry stating, "Then he came to the disciples and said to them, 'Sleep and take your rest later on. See, the hour is at hand, and the Son of Man is betrayed into the hands of sinners. Rise, let us be going; see, my betrayer is at hand'" (Matt. 26:45–46). Suffering is the Christological pattern of normal life.

The writer of Hebrews lets us know that Jesus, in His humanity, learned how to obey through His suffering. The wording in Hebrews is poignant, "In the days of his flesh, Jesus offered up prayers and supplications, with loud cries and tears, to him who was able to save him from death, and he was heard because of his reverence. Although he was a son, he learned obedience through what he suffered. And being made perfect, he became the source of eternal salvation to all who obey him" (Heb. 5:7–9).

Even for the Lord Jesus Christ, in *the days of His flesh, God used His suffering to grow Him in obedience. Being made perfect* is in the passive voice, pointing to the fact that Jesus did not perfect Himself. In this case, God is the agent that acts upon the recipient. *God sanctified Jesus progressively!* This is huge! Jesus depended on the Holy Spirit to grow and maximized all of God's means of growing Him. If Jesus embraced suffering in order to grow in God, being sinless, how much more do we need to submit to God's chiseling work to carve us into the image of Christ?

Peter goes so far as to say,

> For what credit is it if, when you sin and are beaten for it, you endure? But if when you do good and suffer for it you endure, this is a *gracious thing* in the sight of God. For to this you have been called, because Christ also suffered for you, leaving you an example, so that you might follow in his steps. He committed no sin, neither was deceit found in his mouth. When he was reviled, he did not revile in return; when he suffered, he did not threaten, but continued entrusting himself to him who judges justly. (1 Pet. 2:20–23)

The suffering of the believer is the graciousness of God. Do you believe that? We are patterned after the Christological pattern; we understand that we, like Christ, will endure seasons of suffering.

As a pastor, most of my time is spent helping Christians come to terms with difficult circumstances God allows. I've met with couples in crisis, sick people dealing with lengthy seasons of suffering, family grief, singles wrestling with loneliness and jealousy, older believers wrestling with their usefulness—and this is just the tip of the iceberg. When I tell people that one of the reasons they are suffering is because they are being sanctified, many want to punch my face off. And I don't blame them! It is difficult to comprehend

God's graciousness to us through suffering. The reason that they are angry is because they want me to get it to stop. I am always deeply empathetic, but I am also hopeful for their endurance. If God is doing a good work in my people, I don't want it to stop until God is finished blessing them, difficult though it is to bear. I want the power of God to be unleashed in their lives.

God the Great Anchor

Volumes upon volumes have been written in an attempt to reconcile the sovereignty of God with the suffering of man. If God is ruling over the universe, why do bad things happen? I will not attempt to engage those arguments here, but I do want us to see something—namely the anchor.

In the midst of our suffering, there is a constant temptation. "God doesn't care! God isn't good! If God is all-powerful, why would He allow you to go through this?" Essentially, these are darts from the Enemy, thoughts arising as residue from the Fall. One of the most telling statements in the Scriptures is the voice of Job. Job's wife, after great calamity in their lives, says, "Do you still hold fast your integrity? Curse God and die" (Job 2:9). Her words are telling. She makes a bold assertion toward the Lord. Her counsel for suffering could come in many forms toward any of us in suffering. Maybe it's not your wife, but a coworker, or a best friend, or your own imagination; the Enemy can sift you in a number of ways.

In this passage of Job, it's almost like she couldn't fathom God being active in the midst of hardship. Is she telling him to commit suicide? That is extremely harsh. If any of us are to persevere in the midst of pain, we must possess a deep theology of the unmoving character of God that is embedded in the depths of our heart soil.

Job says something that indicates where he is at this point in their suffering: "But he said to her, 'You speak as one of the foolish women would speak. Shall we receive good from God, and shall we not receive evil?' In all this Job did not sin with his lips" (2:10). He basically tells her that she is operating in the realm of unbelief.

Wrestling with God and denying God are two different things. Suffering reveals who is anchoring you at all times. Are your circumstances in life your anchor, or is the God of ages?

Job was willing to think the best of God in the worst of circumstances. We must not let suffering choke out of us the truth about who God is. I am not minimizing our sufferings, and I'm not glorifying them either. The point is that in our journey with Christ under the sovereign omniscient sight of the good Lord, both good and evil will cross our paths. And during both, the Lord remains the same.

Causes of Suffering

That great song "Sovereign" by the incomparable Daryl Coley reminds us of God's sovereignty during seasons of suffering. The Lord uses it to remind me to Whom I am anchored when I endure trials of many kinds. But we must tether ourselves to the anchor with knowledge, not only of the goodness of God, but the danger of evil. So now, we will turn our attention to the various causes of suffering.

Fallen World (The World): If you live in this world, believer or not, you will experience the tragic results of papa Adam. As our representative, Adam's sin brought about the cataclysmic consequences of us being born sinful (Ps. 51). Not only that, it brought about the universal brokenness of our world, now groaning over its condition through natural disasters and the like (Rom. 8). This fundamental flaw passed down to us through Adam creates the potential for suffering of every kind. Not only did Adam and Eve die that day, but all creation was given an expiration date. All suffering finds its root, on some level, in the Fall. It doesn't matter what type of person you are morally or religiously, all are impacted by the Fall. But not all who suffer grow in the midst of it.

Sinful Lifestyles and Systems (The Flesh): Suffering also happens as a consequence of our personal sin and systems of sin that come under our response to the Fall. Because of our natural tendency to sin, given to us from Adam, we suffer under the tyranny of the flesh. Personal sins like greed, pride, or sexual immorality can cause suffering personally. For instance, someone who has a child out of wedlock can find themselves paying child support, which could become a burden to their finances and cause economic suffering. God can redeem the situation, but sometimes the Lord doesn't remove all of the consequences. For the believer, this is called the discipline of the Lord. God will use the most difficult forms of suffering to conform us into the image of Christ. Hebrews talks about this in detail. Peter talks about personal sin that we endure the consequences of as suffering in 1 Peter 2.

Individual sin isn't the only form of suffering we endure, however. No man is an island to himself, and corporate sin creates systemic problems in our society. Sin works like a virus in our communities; one man's sinful disposition can infect his neighbor's. This is why Paul is so aggressive toward false teachers and those who lead others into sin. Systemic sin is contagious like a pathogen, eating away at consciences of individuals. Policies can be made to preserve and promote sin. Just think of the Jim Crow Laws, or Hitler's Aryan Clause. Millions of people suffered, not just individually, but as an entire nation of people.

Everything from racism to socioeconomic oppression can become systems of sin that cause us suffering. But even then, even when all the odds are stacked against us, God can use it to sanctify us until He removes it as an encumbrance to our lives.

Spiritual Warfare (The Devil): Not every type of suffering is the work of the Devil directly, though some might think that is the case. The Bible says that our war is not against flesh and blood, but against an invisible enemy that wreaks havoc on couples, singles, families, sons, and daughters. Satan, the great deceiver, works in the inner city, as well as the suburbs. He lays siege to both bedrooms and boardrooms. The great Liar who tempted Eve in the garden, and Jesus in the desert, does not discriminate. He is an equal opportunity destroyer.

Sometimes when we suffer, it is nothing less than an attack from the Serpent. Though spiritual warfare is related to both the Fall and the flesh, the suffering at the hands of Satan is a unique type of suffering. In these times of suffering, God has given us clear instructions to engage as warriors who put on the whole armor of God (Eph. 6:11–17). As we know by the Word of God, Job endured this type of suffering.

When God Doesn't Take You Out of It

In my sermon prep, I get quite the opportunity to wrestle with the Lord and His Word. Few people are afforded the opportunity to spend hours in focused study the way pastors do—it is truly a gift of grace. But in all of the rest of my life, I wrestle with the implications, application, and transformation of the gospel. The reason being is that if I'm honest, I don't like everything in God's Word. I, like all of you reading, if you're honest too, do not like being told what to do. My like or dislike of what God says doesn't make truth, truth; but Jesus does. Therefore, I need to come into alignment with what the Lord says.

Second Thessalonians 1:11 is one of those verses that doesn't make the struggle any easier. For me what makes this prayer strange is the fact the Thessalonians were in deep levels of suffering. In the midst of all of the suffering that they are going through, Paul, being a good shepherd, seeks to bring grounding in the gospel. Paul, who has done great things by the power of the Holy Spirit, says "To this end we always pray for you, that our God may make you worthy of his calling." One would seem to pass such a prayer without recognizing the nature of this prayer that Paul is praying.

He doesn't pray a triumphalist prayer of deliverance, but something totally different. In a very real sense, he is praying for God to *keep them in the trial.* What the apostle prays is a prayer that some would rebuke in our entitled culture. Someone would say, "I don't receive that," meaning I refuse to remain in circumstances that are uncomfortable. Is it wrong to pray for deliverance? No! However, Paul understood that every hardship we face is God's to shape and transform us.

Christian faithfulness is an act of God. God makes the Christian worthy through the gospel, not something we can attain through moralistic acts of our own volition. The desire here is that God would meet them in their trials in such a way that He causes their worthiness of their calling to be matched by how they handled the suffering in an honorable manner, with His help. For this reason, we should probably see the term *calling* as an allusion to *God's call* to the Thessalonians to share in eschatological salvation.[49] In other words, align your *now* with His *later*.

Paul prays, not for deliverance, but for development. Now, to be honest, if I was suffering like these folks, I might have wanted to punch Paul. For real! Similarly, this prayer for the Thessalonians is strikingly similar to David's praise of how God has dealt with him in times of struggle.

> Answer me when I call, O God of my righteousness! You have given me relief when I was in distress. (Ps. 4:1)

> Answer me when I call, O God of my righteousness! You have relieved me in my distress. (Ps. 4:1 NASB)

Relief here means "to have a momentary or sustained alleviation of trouble or anxiety," as an extension of the meaning to broaden a place, and so have more room to move (Pss. 4:2; 119:32).[50] While in a tight situation, God can loosen. In other words, God can keep you in a trial but give you a sense of deliverance within the trial without removing the trial completely. What a powerful prayer David has here. "Lord, under the pressure of the circumstances, even if You don't take me out, make room for me to feel delivered, even if I am not." It seems as if this is a faithless prayer, but on the contrary, it is a prayer of deep faith.

Paul's prayer is similar for the Thessalonians: "God don't take them out; use them while in their trial." Many of the Psalms overall speak much of God delivering. There is nothing wrong with a prayer for deliverance, but Paul emphasizes the growth of the Christian above that of any other temporal goal.

Jonathan Edwards illustrates this reality in the life of David Brainerd well as he speaks of his emotional and physical challenges while suffering:

> *Thursday, April 16.* Was in bitter anguish of soul, in the morning, such as I have scarce ever felt, with a sense of sin and guilt. I continued in distress the whole day, attempting to pray wherever I went; and indeed could not help so doing, but looked upon myself so vile, I dared not look anybody in the face. Was even grieved that anybody should show me any respect, or at least, that they should be so deceived as to think I deserved it.

> *Friday, April 17.* In the evening, could not but think that God helped me to "draw near to the throne of grace," though most unworthy, and gave me a sense of His favor; which gave me inexpressible support and encouragement.[51]

In my marriage, I began to deal with the struggle of having a very sick wife. Yvette was in need of getting a liver transplant and her condition pre-transplant was worsening to the point where I was forced to imagine being a young widower many times over.

We then lost our first child.

And the text still haunts me, because my doctrine still felt pragmatic and self-centered. I deeply believed that God must heal. Christians stated that, because we were suffering, God owed me and my wife a big church, money, and prosperity. I bought into it in my heart, although it didn't set right with me. God doesn't "owe" anyone a debt, yet in my heart I wanted Him to be indebted because of our pain. I wanted God to owe me, though I owe Him everything.

Later she would receive a liver, have two bouts with infection in the liver, her body would reject the liver—then if that wasn't enough—three bouts with cancer in the new liver, deliver a premature baby, and head back to the inner-city of an even worse city than D.C. to experience the trial of church planting. Wow!

Joy in the Midst of Suffering

Expect this suffering to come, but also expect God to work. Be encouraged that God has counted you worthy to suffer for His name's sake. Even in the book of Acts, Christians viewed suffering differently than we do. In Acts 5:41 the apostles rejoiced in their suffering. We are called to do the same.

Paul furthers his prayer for the Thessalonians in the latter part of verse 11. He prays that while they are in the trial that God "may fulfill every resolve for good and every work of faith by his power" (2 Thess. 1:11). In other words, he prays that the trial won't end their productivity, but that their productivity for the Lord will be maximized. The verb translated *may fulfill* could be used in other contexts to mean "to pay a debt."

But here the sense is rather to complete or finish something already initiated.[52] They will have been purified in such a way that their passions will be unified with God's desired ends. He will bring His goals to pass while they suffer, and that will be their reward. It inherently marries the fact that the suffering is God's will, and that His affection for them is never removed. Finding joy in what God does . . . that is joy alignment. When God changes you through trials, and uses them to strip you bare, you ask for crazy stuff.

I took my sons on a field trip to the Philadelphia Water Works, one of the first city water distribution systems in the modern world.

It was fascinating watching how they built such a sophisticated system for city water distribution in the early 1800s. One of the most interesting facts is the way the water was directed; it depended upon pressure being put on the water to propel it throughout the city. Without the necessary pressure, there wouldn't be as many people served. God allowing trials to place pressure on us doesn't decrease our productivity for Him, but increases it. In the end, His desire is that all of our works would be rooted in faith. The point of our suffering is faith-based works.

On another occasion, while Yvette was hospitalized, we had a Ukrainian medical technician. Yvette shared the gospel with her while in deep physical distress. She was very responsive. However, she desired a Bible in her language. Yvette had a mentor who had a Ukrainian Bible. My wife sent for the Bible and gave it to the tech. She began to weep because of God's great care for her. It bewilders us how God didn't decrease our productivity in these trying times. To be honest, these were some of the most powerful times in our lives.

The "What" of Suffering Versus the "Why"

Fifteen years ago my wife and I experienced our first pregnancy. It was a girl. As we were in our last semester of seminary, we were excited about graduation and a new church. February 5, 2000, I had an OT class that I really needed to go to, and Yvette had an appointment scheduled at the same time as that class. We both agreed that since the pregnancy was going so well that it wouldn't hurt anything for me to miss this one.

While in class, I received a series of frantic calls from Yvette to please call and come to the hospital. I got pulled out of class and found out that at six months of pregnancy the baby had no heartbeat.

As I drove up Highway 75, I wrestled in my heart with the Lord as well as was hopeful that something was wrong with the technology. I got to the hospital and my wife and I wept bitterly at the news. I called the doctor in and we prayed. After that I read John 11 and begged God to resurrect our little girl. The doctor reinitiated the sonogram, but still no breath or heartbeat. Several times we prayed and entreated the Lord for a favorable response, but heaven seemed to be silent.

We induced. Our medical staff prepared a delivery room that was meant for the delivery of a living birth. What should have been a time of excitement became a time of greater pain. The process was quick and swift. Naomi Michelle Mason was delivered. My wife had some complications that determined she needed further attention so they took her to a surgery room and I was left alone with a swaddled stillborn child born premature and lifeless. She looked peaceful, but I was shaken. Looking at her alone, I decided to pick her up and talk to her and pray once again for the breath of life to return. Nothing.

Naomi's death was the first real test of my faith, our faith. What were we to think of God? Why did He allow people that were serving Him to go through something so catastrophic? Did we sin? Was my wife being brought into the consequences of my past sexual sin as a single man? The list of speculation was long.

"Why?" is the question that many of us ask of the Lord when something tragic happens in our lives, or the lives of someone we know. The Bible addresses "What?" far more than "Why?" There is story after story of suffering, but very seldom does the Bible explain why the people are suffering.

Paul says,

> Not only that, but we rejoice in our sufferings, knowing that suffering produces endurance, and endurance produces character, and character produces hope, and hope does not put us to shame, because God's love has been poured into our hearts through the Holy Spirit who has been given to us. (Rom. 5:3–5)

The knowledge of the "what" influences our disposition in our suffering. Rejoicing focuses us on the knowledge of what the Spirit produces in us through suffering. The result is threefold: suffering produces endurance, endurance produces character, and character produces hope.

Suffering Unleashes Endurance: We see this chain of events most clearly in James 1. It is the first stage in the "what" in our suffering. Before we look at endurance I want to explore this reoccurring term, "produces." *Produces* gives us the sense of bringing something out, drawing out potential. It is *unleashing* the power of God in our lives.

Second Peter 1:3 points to the fact that everything we need we already have through the grace of Jesus. That is the gift of positional sanctification. Philippians 2:12 points to the fact that we "work out" our salvation not in or for it, therefore we have what is worked out in us. That is the process of progressive sanctification. He brings out what He placed in us. Everything that God produces is in us through gospel and our spiritual growth progressively brings it out as God works in us.

It reminds me of a sculptor I once knew. I asked him, "How do you sculpt things the way you do?" He said, "Technically, I don't sculpt; I remove. When you look at a stone you see a stone. When I see the stone, I see the image inside of it. I'm merely removing what's in the way of me seeing the image that I see inside of the stone." God through suffering is removing what is in the way of what He put in us through Christ.

I began going to a particular gym, and for the first time in my life, I stuck to the treadmill. While adopting a lifestyle diet, I worked out hard. I did the cardio exercise necessary for better fitness—and it was a monstrous ordeal. The incline on the treadmill was what burned the most calories for me. (I burned between 500–1000.) After some time disciplining myself to the regimen, it became easier to me. As it became easier, I had to increase the challenge to exceed the level of endurance that I had developed from this process before.

Suffering is the believer being thrown onto the treadmill of life challenges. Endurance in the Bible is similar; it means steadfast adherence to a course of action in spite of difficulties and testing.[53] Endurance is the fortitude brought out of us through the grace of God to grow us in gospel endurance. As we go through trials, we develop a greater perseverance to deal with increased challenges. Christians are fragile warriors. We are those who are vulnerable to the fallen world and its elements, but the Lord being inside us by faith makes us durable because of His presence. The more we go through, the stronger in the Lord we become.

Take this story as an example:

Henry Martyn had already done more than his share of missionary service in India when he announced he was going to Persia. Doctors had told him that the heat would kill him if he stayed in India, and the heat in Persia was worse.

Martyn arrived, studied the Persian language and translated the New Testament and Psalms in an amazing nine months. But then was told he must have the Shah's permission to circulate it.

Martyn traveled 600 miles to Tehran, only to be denied permission to see the Shah. He then turned around and made a 400-mile trip to find the British ambassador who gave his credentials and said, "This is all I can do. You will have to present them yourself."

Barely able to stand, Martyn rode at night on the back of a mule and rested in the daytime, protected only by a strip of canvas from the sweltering heat. He was received by the Shah who gave permission for the Scriptures in Persian to be circulated.

Ten days later, in 1812, he died in Turkey. Shortly before he had written in his diary, "I sat and thought with sweet comfort and peace of my God. In solitude my Companion, my Friend, and Comforter."[54]

Looking at the valiant endurance of this faithful Christian soldier, one can see the greatness of the work of God in endurance. The ability to endure hardship is a supernatural power from the great God. To see people survive cancer, amputations, economic losses, families crumble, persecution, and still grow and thrive in the Lord throughout such circumstances is God working.

Endurance Unleashes Character: As God brings out a greater fortitude and capacity to deal with more hardship, God brings out character. Character is the image of Christ that is present in us being made clearer. This is the core of what our growth looks like as a believer. In essence, character means to expose the quality of what is being tested. It indicates the result of being tested, the quality of being approved on the basis of a trial; "the temper of the veteran as opposed to that of the raw recruit."[55] Steadfast endurance leads to the quality of testedness, and this in turn to hope, for the Christian who has been tested has proved God's faithfulness and will surely hope the more confidently.[56]

In other words, character exposes who you are in Christ. It exposes what we are really made of in Him.

> The Greek word for *testing* occurs only in Paul's writings in the New Testament but is part of a word group used of testing or purifying gold by bringing it to the boiling point, thus allowing the lighter minerals (gold is one of the heaviest of metals) to rise to the surface where the goldsmith can skim them off. This is the message in 1 Peter 1:7, where our faith is *refined* or "tested" in the crucible of life to make it purer. In the context of Romans 5:3–5 (as in James and 1 Peter) trials "test" the Christian and give them both endurance and a proven character.[57]

In the heat of suffering, God graces us to endure. Like the smelter of fine metals such as gold, the goldsmith uses the heat under the smelting pot to bring out the impurities in the metals to the top as dross because these metals can't withstand the heat. So, too, God uses our suffering to bring out the impurities in our life and removes them. The smelter knows that the gold or metal is ready to come off of the heat when he sees his facial reflection in the melted metal. When he sees his reflection, he knows that it is now ready to be molded into what he desires. Character, in short, is a greater capacity to reflect who God is in all of our lives. Character is the will to do what's right even when it's hard. "Character is about *will* because it requires a willingness to make tough decisions—decisions that sometimes run contrary to emotion, intuition, economics, current trends, and in the eyes of some, common sense. Having the will to do what's right requires that you determine what's right before the struggle to do what's right ensues."[58]

Character Unleashes Hope: Character that gets sanctified by the gospel gets progressively more stabilized, and is able to focus more effectively on the things of the Lord. Character unleashes hope in suffering. Hope is the joyful expectation of what the Lord has promised. We have lost this as a "now" culture. We have lost confident expectation that is driven by God. Romans 15:13 says, "May the God of hope fill you with all joy and peace in believing, so that by the power of the Holy Spirit you may abound in hope." Paul's prayerful wish for the people of God here flows from chapter 5. Hope is to have a visionary picture of what God has promised, yet not received. We are called to be a glass half-full people not glass half-empty people.

James 1:2–5 reinforces what Paul says in Romans 5 in a more general way, but adds one component. James assures us that the testing of our faith produces endurance. However, if there is any confusion in the midst of our suffering, one must ask for wisdom with full assurance of an answer from God by faith.

Suffering can breed confusion in the best of us—that's where we get the "Why?" Wisdom is God giving clarity in the midst of perplexity. As we grow in wisdom, we are more effective in walking in holiness for our God.

Finally, we realize from all this that God uses our suffering immensely to shape us into the image of Jesus. Many would see suffering as bondage or a leash. However, in the paradoxical kingdom of God, it is actually a place of freedom to see who and what really matters. As disciples of Jesus, we have to use hard times to harness who we really are. As our brokenness is exposed, Jesus is seen. Until the earthen vessel is broken, the treasure within it can't be seen. It is glorious to know that suffering in this life, as a Christian, isn't a denial of who Christ is, but an affirmation. As we go into, come out, and experience in the present our light afflictions, every test of the living God finds us conformed into pure gold for His glory.

CHAPTER 7

Strongholds: Unleashed from the Hindrances to Growth

I really want to cut to the chase. This issue is so key to our growth that I want to just dive into it. So here we go.

Strongholds: everyone has them, but we tend to minimize them. They are the greatest enemy to sanctification because they affect what we believe about faith in God and His Word (though we often fail to see the connection between strongholds and belief). Strongholds bind us to the world, rather than the greatness of the growth that the Lord has for us. Let's get unleashed.

What Is a Stronghold?

Our core passage for addressing strongholds in God's Word is 2 Corinthians 10:3–6:

For though we walk in the flesh, we are not waging war according to the flesh. For the weapons of our warfare are not of the flesh but have divine power to destroy strongholds. We destroy arguments and every lofty opinion raised against the knowledge of God, and take every thought captive to obey Christ, being ready to punish every disobedience, when your obedience is complete.

Strongholds, in Paul's mind, are fleshly arguments that resist the Word of God. Strongholds compete in our minds with God and His Word. These are *unbelieving* belief systems, which inhibit our ability to grow in the sanctifying work of the gospel of our Lord and Christ by faith. In other words, strongholds cause us to have a *faithless* faith, an *anti*-worldview, or an *unbelieving* belief.

"Literally, as a military technical term fortified place, stronghold, bastion; figuratively in the NT as a strong system of philosophy and reasoned arguments *false argument,* opposed to the true knowledge of God."[59] The stronghold isn't necessarily a particular outward sin, but the sinful mind-set that creates an environment for sin. Israel also did what was right in their own eyes/thinking (Judg. 17:6). This is a mind-set that causes sinful actions.

In the OT, a negative stronghold was a *physical fortified place of idolatry.* We will see this in Judges 6 later. The idolatry connected to these strongholds represents, both literally and figuratively, the people of God replacing God and His Word for artifice. The physical stronghold is rooted in a false thinking process about God's character and His Word (spiritual stronghold). Instead of having faith in God, they place it elsewhere. Isn't that true of us today?

My working definition of a stronghold is a mind-set, value system, or thought process that hinders your growth and your exalting Jesus above everything in your life. I don't endorse generally everything David Wilkerson writes, but I believe his definition of strongholds is helpful.

Most of us think of strongholds as bondages such as sexual trespasses, drug addictions, and alcoholism—outward sins we put at the top of a worst-sins list. But Paul is referring here to something much worse than our human measuring of sins.

First of all, he isn't speaking of demonic possession. In my opinion, the devil cannot enter the heart of any over-coming Christian and claim a place in that person. Rather, the figurative meaning of Paul's word *stronghold* in Greek here is "holding firmly to an argument." A stronghold is an accusation planted firmly in your mind. *Satan establishes strongholds in God's people by implanting in their minds lies, falsehoods and misconceptions, especially regarding God's nature.*

For instance, the enemy may plant in your mind the lie that you're unspiritual, totally unworthy of God's grace. He may whisper to you repeatedly, "You'll never be free of your besetting sin. You haven't tried hard enough. You haven't changed. And now God has lost patience with you because of your continual ups and downs."

Satan is the accuser of the brethren, coming against us time after time with his army of accusers, planting demonic lies in our minds. These lies are his stronghold—and if we

don't resist them by God's Word, they will turn into imbed-
ded fears in our minds.

The only weapon that scares the devil is the same one
that scared him in the wilderness temptations of Jesus. That
weapon is the truth of the living Word of God.[60]

Strongholds aren't merely things that *hold onto us,* but are things
that we *hold on to.* James MacDonald's definition is very helpful as
well: "Fortified patterns of thinking that are stubbornly resistant to
God's Word and God's will for us."[61] The word "patterns" imply
bondage, just as the word "unleashed" implies freedom. Strongholds
are the opposite of being unleashed for gospel growth.

Bondage is why strongholds are dangerous for us. Dr. Tony
Evans states that "a stronghold is a mind-set that is viewed as
unchangeable in our minds."[62]

A stronghold is a pattern of unrighteousness that holds you
hostage outside of the will of God. Strongholds result from
something invisible in the spiritual realm cooperating with
something visible in the physical realm, keeping a person
trapped in an addiction or negative life pattern. Overcoming
a stronghold in the physical realm always involves a spiritual
solution, because strongholds always have a spiritual cause.[63]

Most of the sin habits I deal with in ministry are rooted in
strongholds. Shepherding people through these issues requires them
to face the root of their strongholds and exalt Jesus above them. In
all of our lives (including mine), strongholds create blind spots in our
lives that keep us chained to earth instead of heaven. God wants His

people free so that they might be able to have all of His promises and good works lavished on us for His glory.

Typical Strongholds

There are a myriad of stronghold types that people deal with. They are fortified places of fleshly thinking that hold us hostage to sin, and impede our spiritual growth in that area. Remember, it isn't merely the external sin that is the stronghold, but the belief that undergirds that sin which makes it a stronghold. The three following strongholds have some overlap, but may have had a different entry point.

- Personal Strongholds
- Family Strongholds
- Cultural Strongholds

Personal Strongholds: These are strongholds that are reinforced by our personal nurturing. For instance, this stronghold can be emotional in nature. Emotional strongholds are bad mind-sets that have been nurtured by our fallen affections. This could include anger, depression, bitterness, and disappointment. With personal and emotional strongholds, we tend to focus on what has happened to us circumstantially, rather than our belief in what God's Word says about our identity.

For instance, if a young person is sexually abused repeatedly, and the deep pain that it caused never gets addressed biblically, a stronghold will form. Molestation is a heinous sin and is wrong. However, what can happen emotionally after that can cause us to formulate a stronghold in our response. The Enemy will throw at us things like: "God isn't good! Where was He all those years? You have no value!" Victims are then tempted to nurture a false theology of God, and about who God says they are, based on sin that has been perpetrated against them. They can develop a system of belief that affects every area of their lives, exacerbating the pain they experience. Emotional scars are real, and can give birth to spiritual strongholds later in life. It's one of the reasons abuse is so evil.

In essence, an emotional and personal stronghold is something that is perceived as having immediate benefit, but destroys the ability to walk in freedom for the purpose of growth. Take, for example, someone who remains in a toxic relationship. Usually, they are unable to find the faulty belief system that keeps them bound to what's destroying them. Drug addiction is the same thing; sexual addiction is as well. We cling to things that are bad for us; that is the nature of strongholds. A personal stronghold is one that we uniquely own as an individual.

Family Strongholds: Among the fiercest strongholds I've seen are family strongholds. All families are dysfunctional! But the kind of dysfunction I am referring to is when unbiblical patterns emerge in a person's life because of family. If a family doesn't deal with issues biblically, it will affect how one deals with issues the rest of their life.

One of the things that I instituted in our premarital class at Epiphany Fellowship Church is a section on family history. One of the exercises that each couple must complete is to write down the positive and negative qualities of their parents or guardian. We don't do this for the purpose of placing unfair scrutiny on parents, but because we desire to help each member of a new family understand themselves more fully. Once the exercise is complete, they must— with another party that knows them well—ask what characteristics or elements they see in their own lives. Many are shocked at how often negative traits they assign to their parents are manifested in their own life. Family strongholds, for the most part, are strongholds that a family holds in common.

In the Bible we see dysfunction that births strongholds in families that can last over a thousand years. You see Jacob's issues connected to the divide between his father and mother's rearing of him and Esau, which, even after they are reconciled, bled into their children's lives years later. We must face these generational issues biblically if we are going to thrive. Families can be brought out of bondage if they face the stronghold that has ensnared the family.

Cultural Strongholds: Cultural strongholds are blind spots that different (whether the distinguishing trait is ethnic, or socioeconomic, etc.) people groups hold in common as normal, but are antithetical to the gospel. Although they are widely accepted by those who belong to the culture, they must be challenged and destroyed.

I wrote an article on my website about the effects of my upbringing on the current crisis in our culture that has exposed a deep race divide that still exists in the world and in the church. I am deeply knowledgeable that I have strongholds that I need the Lord to address in my life that impact how I view my white brothers and sisters. Here is an excerpt:

> I grew up in an environment in the post-civil rights era when every message from the pulpit was racially charged. I grew up around black nationalists who saw a conspiracy everywhere, and went to one of the oldest historically black colleges in the country, during a time when hip-hop artists had an activist edge to their craft.

In the home where I grew up, I was raised by a mom and dad 50 years older than me. They grew up in the Jim Crow South (South Carolina) and experienced lynching and racism at its height. Growing up in D.C. in the crack era, we were trained to interact with police in a way to keep ourselves safe. I have been racially profiled on more than one occasion.[64]

You can see in this excerpt some overlap between personal, family, and cultural strongholds. My response was to develop some unbiblical framework that didn't leave me upon being justified (positional sanctification). Even to this day, I am actively engaging these issues by confessing and challenging them. These are cultural strongholds that I have to fight in my growth process (progressive sanctification).

Even Peter and Barnabas, in Galatians 2, were faced with cultural strongholds. Cultural strongholds are one of the hardest to break because if they are shared by others in the culture, they can be rationalized through consensus. Breaking a stronghold requires not only personal breakthroughs, but community breakthroughs. To unleash the power of God on a culture requires strength in equal measure with the total size of the culture. Only God can do such things!

Breaking Free Begins with an Encounter with God

No matter how deeply bound anyone is to any given stronghold, through Jesus Christ we are able to overcome. Christ is mightier than the most stubborn heart, and the greatest lie of Satan. On the cross,

Jesus disarmed Satan's devices (Col. 2:15), conquered our every fear and hurt through His love for us (Isa. 53:4; 1 John 4:18). The might of Christ is enough to resurrect our sin-rich hearts heavenward.

In Judges 6, Gideon has an encounter with God that changes the trajectory of his life. In verses 11–32, we see the almost immediate transformation of a life by God when strongholds are properly confronted. In Judges, an unrighteous generation rose up among God's people. Because of the comforts that God had provided for the previous generation, the new generation responded in a way that caused them to become nominal in their commitment to the Lord. You can be guaranteed that when a generation arises that has not been shepherded in the Word of God diligently, strongholds will follow. Entitlement always leads to strongholds.

After Joshua's death, it is clear that God's people didn't disciple their children. As a result, they didn't know the Lord. When discipleship is absent, deep strongholds will arise in a culture. Judges 17:6 states, "In those days there was no king in Israel. Everyone did what was right in his own eyes." In doing so, this shows that they were functioning in deep personal strongholds and it became cultural strongholds. From 2:10 on, it is concluded that their strongholds were rooted in them not knowing the Lord. The word for "know" here is the Hebrew word *yada,* which points to intimacy or relationship. We will see later that they knew *about* the Lord, but they had no *intimacy* or *relationship* with Him.

God makes the journey to confront Gideon's stronghold: "Now the angel of the LORD came and sat under the terebinth at Ophrah, which belonged to Joash the Abiezrite, while his son Gideon was beating out wheat in the winepress to hide it from the Midianites" (Judg. 6:11).

God made the move toward Gideon; Gideon didn't move toward God. A wonderful thing about our great God is that He is willing to engage us even when we refuse to engage Him.

This Angel of the Lord, who is later revealed as the Mighty One Himself, comes in the form of theophany.[65] Although God is all-seeing, He sits under a tree and watches Gideon beat wheat in the winepress. This is unusual, and not just because God appeared in the form of an angel. Ancient people usually threshed their grain by beating the heads of the cut stalks with a flail, discarding the straw, and then tossing the mixture of chaff and grain in the air, allowing the wind to blow away the chaff while the heavier kernels of grain fall to the floor. Normally, this was done on hilltops in order to take advantage of the wind.[66] But because this would have aroused the attention of the marauding Midianites, Gideon resorts to beating the grain under an oak in a sheltered vat used for pressing grapes, which was much harder work than if he were on a hilltop. Gideon used something that was meant for one purpose, for another. God disciplined the children of Israel because of their strongholds.

I call this misuse "functional dysfunction." Functional dysfunction is when we are so spiritually blind that we no longer see the strongholds in our lives. Our strongholds will cause us to do things that a person who is not bound to the same stronghold would notice is dysfunctional. We go on working as if nothing is wrong, learning how to cope by functioning in the midst of gross dysfunction.

An A&E television show called *Hoarders* comes to mind when thinking of functional dysfunction. On this show, people who are addicted to accumulating massive amounts of possessions accumulate so much that their loved ones have to intervene. In most cases, people are so ensnared by the hoarding addiction that they are unaware of how much of their lives are missed out on because of this bondage. One man, for example, had exquisite pieces of art, but they were destroyed because of his hoarding. In another case, a woman became so distraught after her mother died, she kept so much trash in her house, that her husband and children were driven away by the unlivable environment. She was so committed to the trash in the house, that she has never seen her own grandkids. These hoarders find ways to rationalize choosing literal trash over things that are far more precious. They gain functional dysfunction.

As bad as this is, it doesn't stop the God of all mercy from pursuing us. God meets Gideon in his stronghold. In other words, God doesn't wait for Gideon to get it right before He pursues him; He pursues Gideon because He knows that Gideon can't get it right. We are helpless to come out of our sin without God. This is how God demonstrates His love for us. He sent Jesus before our justification, and our sanctification works the same way, God moves on us. The simple fact that you are reading this now is because God is pursuing you; He hasn't given up on you!

I have three boys and they are the kings of interruptions. They don't care who is talking to me, they will respectfully find a way to get my attention. Many times, their interruptions are divinely orchestrated moments. When they need me, they need me. It doesn't matter if dad is at church or at home. My favorite is the tug of my coat. When my five-year-old wants me, he will tug my clothing and say, "Excuse me, Dad." Nothing delights me more.

The Lord does the same to us. He orchestrates divine interruptions to accent His importance in our lives. Often, He ensures the pull of our coats to get our attention.

This Ain't You

How in the world does God call a man that is hiding from his enemies and functioning in functional dysfunction, a mighty man of valor? God doesn't call us to Him based on *us*, but based on *Himself*.

From a human standpoint, God is the worst picker of people. People that most of us would choose usually have some type of résumé that would dictate that they are qualified for what we want or need them for.

One of the powerful ways He does this in grace as shown in Gideon's life is letting Gideon know who He is or can be in connection with the King of kings. God wants Gideon to know that what He is doing *ain't him*. He pulls Gideon's coattails by calling out his name and affirming His presence with him. The nickname that God gives him is very strange. He calls him "mighty man of valor." The NET Bible says "courageous warrior." It also can mean, mighty warrior, valiant soldier, i.e., mighty hero who is very capable of defense or attack (1 Sam. 2:4; Ps. 33:16), prominence, one of standing, a community leader of influence (Ruth 2:1; Ezra 7:28); the best of the fighting men (Josh. 10:7).[67]

In the first analysis, might and mighty men were causes for celebration in the OT. During much of the biblical period Israel was in a heroic age. Thus the feats and exploits of her champions were causes for delight and storytelling. Such an exploit was that of David's three mighty men as they broke through the Philistine lines to bring him water from Bethlehem (1 Chron. 11:15–19).[68]

Our Great and Mighty God utilizes His résumé, not ours. He'll go on a holy rant to remind us who He is. God's passion to use us is wrapped up not in our greatness, but in His. He even says in Deuteronomy 7,

> It was not because you were more in number than any other people that the LORD set his love on you and chose you, for you were the fewest of all peoples, but it is because the LORD loves you and is keeping the oath that he swore to your fathers, that the LORD has brought you out with a mighty hand and redeemed you from the house of slavery, from the hand of Pharaoh king of Egypt. Know therefore that the LORD your God is God, the faithful God who keeps covenant and steadfast love with those who love him and keep his commandments, to a thousand generations. (vv. 7–9).

There it is!

Look at Jesus' world-changing, disciple-making roster. Jesus called religious skeptics, businessmen, Hebrew fundamentalists, thieves, thugs, a shady government worker, radical Jews, mama's boys, spoiled rich kids, prostitutes, outcasts, aristocrats, legalists, and licentious people into one crew to represent Him. It is mind-boggling that Jesus would choose the willing, not merely the wealthy. What makes the gospel narrative of our lives so great is not anything that we have done, but all that He has done.

When I used to hit the basketball courts, I would either go with a solid crew who could play, or wait and choose the good players from the losing team. My desire was to run the court as long as possible, with one team. God, on the other hand, goes to the court of life and scouts the players with absolutely no potential. He chooses losers, slow players, poor shooters, and folks who never hustle. But after choosing them to be on His squad, He gives them what they need for the game of life. He receives all the more glory by winning with that team, as opposed to if He gathered the NBA all-stars. God who begins a good work in us (positional sanctification) is faithful to continue it (progressive sanctification).

How Dare Us!

Gideon had a response to God that isn't far off from many of us who are stuck in our own stronghold.

And Gideon said to him,

> "Please, sir, if the LORD is with us, why then has all this happened to us? And where are all his wonderful deeds that our fathers recounted to us, saying, 'Did not the LORD bring us up from Egypt?' But now the LORD has forsaken us and given us into the hand of Midian." (Judg. 6:13)

In essence, he says,

- Where is God?
- Why are we suffering?
- What happened to His great power?
- How is it that the Lord doesn't seem to care for us any longer?

It is interesting that Gideon blames God because of where his life and the life of the people of God are. It is, in fact, their fault because of where things are. It is their disposition toward the Lord that has created the issues that they are facing.

Many of us question God because of our circumstances, rather than questioning ourselves. When functioning within dysfunction, it is difficult to perceive God's promises. But we shouldn't question God's faithfulness if we are trapped in a stronghold; it is far more likely that something else lurks beneath the surface.

If the Lord is with us, why has all this happened to us? (6:13). Gideon's reference to Yahweh as the God of the Exodus here implies they are having trouble perceiving Him as the God who will take care of them in the land of Canaan. Judging by Gideon's cynical questions, Yahweh has been either apathetic or impotent to intervene in Israel's present crisis. Thus, they turned to local gods of the Canaanites to take care of them. These are the gods on whom one depended for the fertility of livestock, the soil, and their own wives. They have forgotten Yahweh's explicit declarations and covenant promises to satisfy their needs at *every* level, including securing the well-being of individuals and families (Deut. 7:6–16).[69] It isn't the Lord who placed them in the current calamity, but because they forsook the Lord (Judg. 6:1) that they are ensnared. Many times, when we are feeling the effects of our sin, we find ourselves blaming God and others for what we have created for ourselves.

Demands a Radical Commitment to Face Strongholds Head-On

One of the great things about being in a relationship with God is that He calls us to confrontation. Confrontation is dealing honestly with our brokenness and sin with truth.

Isn't it ironic how prideful we tend to be when we ignore sin? Ignoring our sin isn't a valiant act, but a cowardly one. Jesus' death on the cross is God displaying His commitment to confronting us on the realest level. The cross of Christ Jesus is God's commitment to confront us and heal us at the same time by faith. Jesus didn't run from our shame, but toward it, and took it fully on in order that we wouldn't have to. Strongholds can in most cases be very shameful places in our lives. Since Christ Jesus already engaged these places of deep brokenness and pain in our lives on the cross, we have no embarrassment to fear. We can see that dealing with our strongholds is a powerful grace from the living God to recognize and engage. One of the greatest freedoms of being a Christian is the freedom to deal with our issues head-on. Because Christ has already dealt with them, we are promised the grace of His victory. Have no fear; confront your strongholds.

I had a vicious cold recently. It put me out of commission for almost a week and a half. I found out that it was a virus, and because it was a virus, there was only so much I could do. Although I blew my nose, drank plenty of liquids, and got rest, I could only address the symptoms of the virus—not the virus itself. The virus was located much deeper than I was able to reach. Therefore, the doctor ordered medication to help my body fight off what it was struggling to fight off in itself.

Whenever dealing with strongholds we have to go to the root. Dealing with a symptom only impacts the surface level of a stronghold, but the virus that supports the stronghold will remain. God empowers us by the Spirit to fight our strongholds like medication that strikes at the virus level.

Gideon's encounter with the Lord God gave him a basic confidence necessary to confront his strongholds. God commands Gideon to go and tear down the altar! I believe that this is key. Being commanded helps us to understand the mandatory mandate that is on us to deal with our strongholds. In addition, it also infers empowerment.

He first calls for the pulling down of the altar of Baal and then he will call for the cutting down of the Asherah. Both gods were set up for them to worship because of what they were believed to provide. What's funny is that they were committed to these gods in the midst of horrible conditions. Both gods were believed to create fruitfulness; however, they brought no such thing. Many times the Enemy will dupe the believer into thinking that strongholds are giving more than they actually can. Satan is the king of over-promising and under-delivering.

Baal was believed to be the weather god of fertility, and Asherah was the goddess of fertility. These two together presented a lethal combination for the people of God. It had deep sexual connotations. That is why the high places were so huge in this day. People would have sex on the high places to incite Baal to make it rain and fertilize Asherah. And the fruit of their union would be crops for the people. Their lack of faith in the living God caused them to get into deeper bondage than they had bargained for.

> While Yahweh had demonstrated his cosmic sovereignty through the wonders he had performed in Egypt (Deut. 4:32–40), and his role as Israel's national God by entering into relationship with them at Sinai (cf. Judg. 6:8–10), during the period of the judges the Israelites apparently had difficulty conceiving of him as a personal and family deity.
>
> Thus, they turned to local gods of the Canaanites to take care of them at this level. These are the gods on whom one depended for the fertility of livestock, the soil, and their

own wives. They have forgotten Yahweh's explicit declarations and covenant promises to satisfy their needs at *every* level, including securing the well-being of individuals and clans (Deut. 7:6–16).[70]

In essence, they turned to unbelief. Unbelief in the living God in any area of our lives always leads to strongholds. When this happens it impacts our ability to grow overall or in an area of our life and fellowship with the living God. We must go to the places of unbelief in our lives and confront them.

What caused me to question the character of God in this area? How has this unbelief impaired my commitment to Jesus? Why do I view this stronghold the way that I have? When did I begin to revel in unbelief in God in this area? All of these are key questions for us. Inside of these questions lies the rebooting of our spiritual growth in the good Lord.

In dealing with strongholds it involves dealing with the deepest and darkest places that are in your life. You cannot ignore your past and expect for your life to be different. You must face your past with the gospel.

When David went after Bathsheba, he confronted his unbelief in the God who had provided so much for him. That is why Nathan said to David,

"You are the man! Thus says the Lord, the God of Israel, 'I anointed you king over Israel, and I delivered you out of the hand of Saul. And I gave you your master's house and your master's wives into your arms and gave you the house of Israel and of Judah. And if this were too little, I would add to you as much more. Why have you despised the word of the Lord, to do what is evil in his sight? You have struck down Uriah the Hittite with the sword and have taken his wife to be your wife and have killed him with the sword of the Ammonites. Now therefore the sword shall never depart from your house, because you have despised me and have taken the wife of Uriah the Hittite to be your wife.'" (2 Sam. 12:7–10)

Yahweh told him, "If what I given you wasn't enough, I would have done more."

We underestimate God.

Our strongholds are, at their core, unbelief. The antidote, therefore, to strongholds is a strong belief. God is a good God who, as David would later say, "The Lord God is a sun and shield; the Lord bestows favor and honor. No good thing does he withhold from those who walk uprightly" (Ps. 84:11). Do we believe that? Good is good from *His perspective*, not ours.

Conclusion

One of the things that I love about God is that when He challenges us to grow through removal, He replaces that which He removes. Our Lord does not merely take from us but He also gives generously. In Jesus, all of the promises of God are lavished on us (2 Cor. 1:20). Where Gideon used to worship idols, God tells him to build an altar to Him in the same places where he used to worship false gods and walk in broken commitment to stronghold. He replaces a god with God.

Building up in the place where there was a stronghold is simply having the Word of God replace an existing false belief system. Because strongholds are stubborn value systems that we have built in our minds, we must place a biblical value system in its place. If the goodness of God is an issue for the believer, then the Bible's teaching on God's goodness is the altar to build in the place of idols. If sex is an issue, biblical sexuality must replace counterfeit teachings on sex and pleasure. Many of us have a law-based view of God's Word. Faith in the gospel frees us to enjoy again. Since God is the creator of enjoyment, it changes our worldview on that issue, and we find a greater sense of freedom in Jesus Christ. The more we develop a Christian worldview, the more effectively we can grow in the Lord. This goes back to the chapter on the Word of God as a means of our growth. As the Lord grows us by faith in the gospel, we must seek the means that He uses by the Spirit to grow us.

If we are going to walk in our God-ordained growth in Jesus, we must not be reluctant to confront our strongholds with belief in God's Word. Jesus Christ has already given us the victory through His death and resurrection by faith. Let's be unrelentingly committed to being unleashed for gospel growth by dealing with that which binds us.

CHAPTER 8

Marriage and Spiritual Growth

For most married couples, you don't need a Bible verse to tell you that marriage works on the soul, like almost no other means of grace. Martin Luther said, "Before I was married the bed was not made for a whole year and became foul with sweat. But I worked so hard and was so weary I tumbled in without noticing it."[71] Marriage as an institution created by God is one of the most wonderful in the world. Because of the Fall and corruption in the world, this great institution finds itself consistently in great flight.

There is no other issue that fills my counseling calendar as I pastor God's people than marriage. Sitting in session after session, I am bombarded with people who see the validity of their perspective on their spouse's sinfulness. Rather than owning and mortifying their own sinful contribution to the state of the brokenness in their marriage, blame-shifting is the norm. Rather than unity, disunity is commonplace. Gospel growth is at a stalemate, for both believing husbands and wives who are driven by their need to be understood by their spouse.

Even in my own marriage (of almost two decades), we continue to wrestle in our practical oneness with Jesus and one another as we are being conformed into the image of Christ. It is an ever-growing battle to partner with my wife so that we see our marriage as an individual and unified journey with God.

We have an active role in marriage as we partner with the covenant Maker and Keeper on our marriages, not a passive one. This means, as it relates to our responsibility to work toward gospel growth, we cannot ignore the strongholds in our marriage.

But, just like every area of sanctification, marriage is something that happens to us by grace of God, and not in our strength. Martin Luther infers that marriage is the ultimate tool for sanctification. This is another way God conforms us into His image.

Luther talks extensively about the changes that had to take place in his life because of marriage. And the Bible itself uses words like *submission* and *sacrifice* to mark the dispositions of a husband and wife. Both husbands and wives need to look to the Lord Jesus Christ, because in doing so, the two become helpful to the spiritual growth of the other. Most of all, we need our mind renewed in this area in order that we may approach marriage with a robust understanding of God's work in us in the midst of it.

Many couples are frustrated because they want to . . .

- Conform their spouse to their image
- Get their spouse to do what they want

- Measure their happiness by their spouse meeting their needs
- Use what the spouse wants to get what they want from them

Rather than:

- Serve God by serving their spouse
- Be committed to the growth of their spouse
- Be a tool in God's hand for their spouse's growth
- Illustrate who Jesus is with the church

Oneness (Gen. 2)

My wife and I attended Family Life conferences in the past. Family Life is a wonderful ministry that is dedicated to serving families to be equipped to honor God in every area of the family. One of their strengths is marriage. As we attended these events, we kept hearing a word that stuck with us: "oneness." *Oneness* is a term that is rooted in the pre-Fall of creation, the idea of "one flesh." Oneness in marriage equips couples to grow in true intimacy, connection, and purpose—and experience closeness for a lifetime.[72] Oneness is rooted in the prophetic voice of the first man in the biblical epilogue.

Adam made a statement after Eve was created and God brought her to Him:

> "This at last is bone of my bones and flesh of my flesh; she shall be called Woman, because she was taken out of Man." (Gen. 2:22)

Then God said:

"Therefore a man shall leave his father and his mother and hold fast to his wife, and they shall become one flesh. And the man and his wife were both naked and were not ashamed." (Gen. 2:24–25)

Eve was so fine that Adam prophesied about marriage. He began to speak of parental relationships before there were human parents in existence.

The NET Bible note here gives us great clarity of what is meant by this powerful idea for the first man and woman and all who would come after them.

The phrase "one flesh" occurs only here and must be interpreted in light of v. 23. There the man declares that the woman is bone of his bone and flesh of his flesh. To be one's "bone and flesh" is to be related by blood to someone. For example, the phrase describes the relationship between Laban and Jacob (Gen. 29:14); Abimelech and the Shechemites (Judg. 9:2; his mother was a Shechemite); David and the Israelites (2 Sam. 5:1); David and the elders of Judah (2 Sam. 19:12); and David and his nephew Amasa (2 Sam. 19:13; see 2 Sam. 17:2; 1 Chron. 2:16–17). The expression "one flesh" seems to indicate that they become, as it were, "kin," at least legally (a new family unit is created) or metaphorically. In this first marriage in human history, the woman was literally formed from the man's bone and flesh. Even though later marriages do not involve such a divine surgical operation, the first marriage sets the pattern for how later marriages are understood and explains why marriage supersedes the parent-child relationship.[73]

Oneness is both a position and a practice. Even prior to the Fall, Adam viewed the leaving and cleaving concept as something that needed to be volitionally engaged for the good of the marital union. "The narrator is using hyperbole to emphasize the change in perspective that typically overtakes a young man when his thoughts turn to love and marriage."[74]

Adam also says *cleave*, "it has the basic idea of 'stick with/to' (e.g., it is used of Ruth resolutely staying with her mother-in-law in Ruth 1:14). In this passage it describes the *inseparable* relationship between the man and the woman in marriage as God intended it."[75] Therefore, the union was meant to be an enduring one in the midst of adjustments for both the wife and the husband. Marriage is an adjustment. For two totally different people with unique experiences, oneness is difficult to achieve.

The narrator of Genesis then communicates something very intriguing about their makeup in being able to live in light of this oneness: "And the man and his wife were both naked and were not ashamed" (2:25). Naked and unashamed is rich with meaning.

In this context [naked] signifies either innocence or integrity, depending on how those terms are defined. There is no fear of exploitation, no sense of vulnerability. But after the entrance of sin into the world, nakedness takes on a negative connotation. It then is connected with the sense of vulnerability, shame, exploitation, and exposure (such as the idea of "uncovering nakedness" either in sexual exploitation or in captivity in war). . . . The word conveys the fear of exploitation or evil—enemies are put to shame through military victory. It indicates the feeling of shame that approximates a fear of evil.[76]

Sin ruined everything.

The Beast and the Blessing

Of course, all of our problems stem from Genesis 3. It is interesting that the Fall happened in the context of marriage. Satan didn't attack Adam until he got married. This is not to say at all that singles aren't attacked by Satan, and this isn't to say that singles don't find great struggle in the process of being conformed to the image of Christ. However, there isn't anyone I know who is married that wouldn't quickly say that marriage has made them acutely aware of themselves and need for growth on a deeper level.

Satan's attack on marriage was an attack on the glory of God in all creation:

> What Satan tries to get us to do is relinquish our rule by handing it over to him and by deceiving us into believing that he has authority. Or else he tries to get us to rule poorly based on our own judgments and distorted worldviews. It isn't until we rule with wisdom under the comprehensive rule of God that we will become the rulers he intended.[77]

When attacking Adam and Eve, Satan zoomed in on their oneness. Adam and Eve being on the same page impacted the polarity of the universe.

Satan came against the marital order by engaging Eve and not Adam. Paul reveals that created order (not value distraction) existed prior to the Fall (1 Cor. 11:1–3; 1 Tim. 2:13). This is not a view of importance or value, but distinction and function. When we are led to try and be more or less than God created us to be, we can be sure we are being led by the Enemy. We find our value in who God created us to be, not in view of being the master of our fate or the captain of our soul. On the contrary, it is deep bondage. This goes for both men and women.

When Satan tempted Eve, he was defying God's created design. In Matthew 4 we see Satan tempting the New Adam (Jesus) to function outside of His role. That temptation was the same for Eve. Eve allowed the lies of the Enemy to forfeit her role before God. Adam, by eating from the tree under the leadership and deception of his wife, was to live below his calling as the first vice regent and federal head of creation (Rom. 5 and 1 Cor. 15). Prior to the Fall, they were both to function as distinct co-equal vice regents who would have dominion over all of creation. When husbands and wives refuse to operate together, they forfeit their birthright under the living God. Moreover, because of their forfeiture, they gain sinfulness and lose everything. Satan gains a larger access to earth through the Fall of man. Satan deceives us in marriage to give up what is rightfully ours to give him access to what God has banned him from.

Before they were naked and unashamed. Now they are naked and ashamed! They live under emotional vulnerability, mistrust, insecurity, and divisiveness. To put it in terms we might better understand in light of this book, they are trapped in new strongholds. God told the woman that the Fall ruptured her relationship with her husband; the curse was a negative desire for her husband, and that he will rule her (Gen. 3:16). "The LORD also declares that a struggle, a conflict would emerge between the man and the woman. She will desire to control him, but he will dominate her instead."[78] This passage is a judgment oracle. It announces that conflict between man and woman will become the norm in human society. It does not depict the NT ideal, where the husband sacrificially loves his wife, as Christ loved the church, and where the wife recognizes the husband's loving leadership in the family and voluntarily submits to it. Sin gives birth to a power struggle between the man and the woman.

However in Christ, humanity can overcome the strongholds passed down through the dysfunctional family legacy after the Fall. "In Christ, man and woman call a truce and live harmoniously (Eph. 5:18–32)."[79] After the Fall, marriage became a kingdom of coups d'état, where the struggle for power will be constant. However, the great and mighty God, while speaking to the Serpent, in the midst of this judgment oracle gives hope to His wayward children, looking forward to the coming Christ, saying,

> "I will put enmity between you and the woman, and between your offspring and her offspring; he shall bruise your head, and you shall bruise his heel." (Gen. 3:15)

The pre-incarnate One foreshadows the removal of the demonic dominion of the Serpent. He will come and restore, as the new Adam, a new rule that will give man and woman the ability to fight the imbalance brought about by the Fall. As the New Adam, Jesus isn't merely a man, and "like God"; He is God, yet man. Now in marriage, redeemed men and women are empowered to live under the authority of Christ, fighting the fleshly tendencies of the sin of the first Adam.

The Source of Marital Growth

I have had the honor of officiating tons of weddings. As I listen to them speak to me in the first year into the marriage, they say to me, "Pastor, I don't see how people make it without Jesus in marriage." They always get a resounding amen from me.

In order for marriage to work according to God's design, it takes two whole people to achieve oneness with Jesus, by faith, to move forward. Because the gospel makes us whole, husbands and wives who know Jesus have what is necessary to glorify Christ in marriage. Our goal as individuals in Christ is to glorify God through bearing much fruit (John 15:8). In marriage, bringing two individuals to become one, the goal is the same (Eph. 5).

As an illustration of Jesus' relationship with the church, marriage is supposed to be a reflection of the church having been conformed to the image of Christ. Jesus has made the church positionally one with Himself already (John 17; Eph. 2). As members of the body of Christ, Jesus is the source of our growth as our head. Husbands and wives must remember this in marriage. Their spouse is not their source of growth, happiness, and security. Although the Lord uses husbands and wives in many ways, at the end of the day, Jesus is the source of the believer—period.

Marriages become deeply troubled when spouses expect their companion to do and be something that they were never intended to do. We must be constantly reminded that sex, cleaning, providing, working, children, houses, etc., in marriage isn't that on which we need to be centered. Jesus is the center.

Couples must be committed to Jesus being formed in their spouse. Keller states it well:

Romance, sex, laughter, and plain fun are the by-products of this process of sanctification, refinement, glorification. Those things are important, but they can't keep the marriage going through years and years of ordinary life. What keeps the marriage going is your commitment to your spouse's holiness. You're committed to his or her beauty. You're committed to his greatness and perfection. You're committed to her honesty and passion for the things of God. That's your job as a spouse. Any lesser goal than that, any smaller purpose, and you're just playing at being married.[80]

When couples are feasting on Jesus, they approach marriage with the constant reality of their need for Jesus and His work for the marriage partnership to be a community of conformity. We have already spoken about the filling of the Spirit, but I find it interesting that before Paul speaks of marriage in Ephesians 5, he talks about being filled with the Spirit. Spirit-filled Christianity is the power source for a healthy marriage.

The Husband's Commitment to Sanctification

Jesus has restored to men the ability to be who God has called them to be (see Eric Mason, *Manhood Restored,* Nashville: B&H Publishing Group). He is empowering men by the Spirit to walk in biblical manhood, but also to flesh out their identity in biblical marriages. Now that we have been redeemed, now that we have exchanged our old identity and put on Christ, we are called by the Lord to walk in the faithfulness of Jesus. This process runs parallel with our sanctification.

In marriage, the barometer for how well we are growing is selflessness versus selfishness. We will engage a short list of biblical parameters that are some of the gauges for how we are progressing as husbands and then as wives.

Love: Ultimately Jesus sets the tone for men as the New Adam. Jesus embraces His role as the new and true husband, and dies to sanctify His wife. His death sets her aside and sets her up to win in order that He may present to God a perfect bride (Eph. 5:25–26). Although, ultimately, Jesus does this for both genders who are members of His bride the church, the husband should find particular insights by looking to Jesus as Paul instructs. So, what is love?

In the big picture of Ephesians 5, Jesus' relationship with the church is mystery revealed. Within the framework of this mystery, we see that the relationship between husband and wife is an illustration of that eternal relationship. Jesus doesn't merely expose her sin, but gives His life to aid her in the mire of her sinfulness. Therefore the text states, "Husbands, love your wives, as Christ loved the church and gave himself up for her, that he might sanctify her, having cleansed her by the washing of water with the word" (Eph. 5:25–26). He loves the church in these verses by His death (gave Himself up for her), and by perfecting her (sanctifying her). This selfless love is a selfless and enduring commitment to care about and benefit another person by righteous, truthful, and compassionate thoughts, words, and actions.[81] Dying is self-explanatory, but perfecting her needs a bit of explanation. Jesus has perfected the church positionally. Husbands *don't* sanctify their wives (nor do wives their husbands, Jesus has done that through the word of the gospel). However, husbands, from a practical standpoint, act as the hands and feet of Jesus in marriage to be a means of grace for the wife's growth.

Servant-Leadership: Because wives, like husbands, need to grow spiritually, God uses the husband as a servant leader to continue to act as a conduit of grace of the gospel to point the wife to her washing from sin through Jesus through the Word of God.

Let's take a look at the washing metaphor in the text. Now, one wouldn't wash someone they loved in a coarse manner. When I used to hand-wash dishes, I remember there was a scrub pad for pots that could puncture my skin. I would not imagine using that on my wife to wash her. Husbands are to graciously wash their wife. Even Colossians 3:19 states that husbands shouldn't be harsh toward the wife. Harsh means, make something turn sour, to cause bitter feelings, embitter, make bitter, literally *make bitter;* of waters *cause to be undrinkable,*[82] and to be or become marked by strong resentment or cynicism. In context, the language stresses the act of the husband doing something to the wife to put her in a place of resentment.

Bitterness is the sin of the fermentation of anger, or unaddressed unforgiveness. The Bible doesn't condone every way a wife might respond, but it does make it clear that the husband is responsible for gracious interaction. This doesn't mean that husbands don't engage hard issues with the wife in marriage (passivity), because the issue is not whether hard issues will be addressed, but how.

What does this have to do with being conformed to the image of Jesus? Well, the husband is supposed to be a supporter of the growth of his wife as a means of grace in her life, not her destruction. Nourishing and cherishing (Eph. 5:29) are the antithesis of harshness. The husband must provide spiritual food and place the wife in environments where spiritual food is being dispensed.

For instance, if the husband and wife are attending a church and the husband is being blessed by it, but his wife is having a hard time, the husband must consider the wife's spiritual condition and receptivity before his own. Husbands must know the condition of his wife's soul so that he may administer what is needed for her growth. Because the wife and the husband are one, the husband must take concern for the wife's growth as he would attending to himself.

Delicate Matters: When I first got married, my wife used to have a saying to help me be more tender toward her. She would face-tiously say, "Babe, I'm a flower!" I would know at that moment that I needed to deal with her in a more delicate manner.

Cherish is a term men need a lot of help in order to apply. God grows us as we are being used as tools for our wife's growth (and vice versa). Men, you will grow when you serve for your wife's growth! Cherish means to strictly impart warmth—hence cherish, comfort, tenderly care for.[83] Growing as a husband in this regard is important for the wife's growth.

This is also explained in 1 Peter 3:7, "Likewise, husbands, live with your wives in an understanding way, showing honor to the woman as the weaker vessel, since they are heirs with you of the grace of life, so that your prayers may not be hindered." It is funny that Peter gives wives six verses to communicate their role, while he gives the husband one. However, the seriousness of the husband's charge in marriage is weighty and stern. A husband can have his prayers (growth) hindered by harsh treatment of the wife. God protects the wife from a foolish husband by closing heaven's windows if he treats her unjustly. Therefore, he must live with the wife in an understanding way. This connects to Ephesians 5, Colossians 3, and

Malachi 2. God is very concerned about the husband's commitment to serve his spouse's growth.

One very practical way to obey God's command to cherish our wives is how we communicate with her. I know at times, I have measured my speech toward my wife based on the public. In other words, how would others perceive my treatment of my wife if I was speaking to her in public? If my verbiage could be construed as domineering and insensitive, then I am not helping her grow, but embittering her.

Not only do husbands aid in the growth of the wife by how he communicates to her, but how he receives and understands her. Stu Weber, in his book *Tender Warrior,* has a chapter called, "Does Anyone Here Speak 'Woman'?" That chapter alone has helped the sanctification of my wife and me in ways that I am still being blessed by. Listen to him drop practical gospel knowledge:

> That, my friend, is a man's responsibility. He is the one who must take the initiative and learn how to speak Woman. He is the one who must weather the awkward stuttering of lines from a woman's phrase book. So many give up after a few faltering, self-conscious attempts. But real men don't have that option. Real men "remain under" the responsibility, absorb the setbacks, swallow their pride, and keep trying. Real men stay and stay and stay. When a man takes the risk and the initiative to learn his wife's language and understand her deepest needs, he is living out the heart of masculinity. Remember the ancient Hebrew words for man and woman? "Piercer" and "pierced." It's up to the husband to take the initiative, to open up his wife's heart, to speak

her language, to penetrate her world. And as we mentioned earlier, sexual relations represent only the tiniest portion of that huge reality.[84]

Use Your Ears, Not Your Mouth: Let's get even more personal. One of the many painful lessons I continue to learn in helping my wife in her journey with Jesus is feeling the need to fix her. She will begin to unload her woes on me. As a man, I'm thinking, *Oh no, this plane is going to have to land or I'm going to die.* And like a dummy, I interject in the middle of her distress, looking for an exit for myself, rather than sacrificial service. I begin to solve her problem with robust theological truths and with practical prowess . . . *not.*

As I begin to open my mouth, I can see her shutting down.

Therefore, growing in my marital bilingual communication, I have learned to remain quiet, nod, stroke her hand, give timely grunts, and apologize for what she is dealing with. At the end, she either solves the problem (by the Holy Spirit guiding her) or she will thank me for listening. Later, after some time listening she may ask me, "Babe, what do you think?" I found my ears are the key to her heart and growth.

Sanctification in marriage is an eternal art and science. As men we need to understand this and lead through all these means for the growth of the wife and our own. Just as Jesus seeks to present the church without spot or wrinkle through His sacrificial death, so also a husband his wife.

The Wife's Commitment to Sanctification

Jesus has also restored to women the ability to be who God has called them to be. He is empowering women by the Spirit to walk in biblical womanhood, to flesh out their identity in biblical marriages as wives. Now that they have been redeemed, now that they too have exchanged their old identity and put on Christ, wives are called by the Lord to walk in the faithfulness of Jesus. This process, just like the husband's, runs parallel with our sanctification. And like the husband, in marriage, the barometer for how well they are growing is measured in accordance with God's Word. We will examine a practical list of parameters that serve as gauges for how wives are progressing in their journey to be conformed into the likeness of Christ.

What Is Submission? Bunny Wilson, in her classic book *Liberated by Submission,* challenges women in the beauty of biblical submission:

> You can wait patiently for the Fourth of July to arrive to enjoy the brilliant fireworks. Or you can mention the word "submission" to a group of women! Their verbal response is likely to be just as explosive and colorful as any summer sky-rockets or sparklers you could ever hope to see. Few words in the English language (or in any other language) evoke such a controversial response as the word "submission."[85]

The above quote is the opening lines that Wilson uses to communicate a common experience. I can remember preaching through the book of Ephesians and arriving at Ephesians 5. When the word *submission* came up, the room went silent.

Even more recently, a more controversial verse we engaged was 1 Corinthians 14. What is funny is "tongues and prophecy" took a backseat to "women keep silent." I could remember the storm cloud that formed over 1632 Diamond Street as we read those verses.

When we approached 33–36 I watched the room fill with both horror and laughter as we read the ancient text. Because we preach expositionally, we deal with all the contents of the Bible. We don't avoid the difficult passages; we plow through the text by faith.

Practical Submission: Biblical submission has practical limits. The wife's submission to a husband expires practically if he is leading her into sin and/or abusing her. She must not submit to him in those situations. That isn't a trial that will grow her, but a kind of evil suffering that will destroy her.

Just as love in Ephesians 5 is the centerpiece of the text for the husband's responsibility in glorifying God in oneness of marriage, so also is submission for the wife. Verse 21 calls for the submission of *all* Christians—husbands, wives, singles, sons, and daughters—to the Holy Spirit! Therefore, the power of the Spirit empowers both the husband and the wife to submit to their roles in marriage. This is good news for both.

Eve Redeemed: Wives are empowered by the Spirit to live in light of their powerful God-ordained role. For a woman not to walk in biblical submission to her husband, she will live in bondage under her mother, Eve. But as "Eve redeemed," female disciples of Jesus, in marriage, are contributors to the spiritual growth of their husband. Just as husbands can be a means of grace in the lives of their wives, wives also can be a means of grace in the life of their spouse.

Submission is a powerful term. The Devil has sought to destroy this term by emptying it of its powerful value. One of the most powerful images in the Bible is that the wife's submission to the husband should look like that of a devout disciple of Jesus Christ. "By using the same verb 'submit' (a middle voice in the original language) Paul stresses the willing character of the church's submission to Christ, and thus underscores what has already been asserted in v. 22 about the free and voluntary nature of the wife's subordination to her husband."[86] This is done by the wife volunteering to coming under the headship of her husband. Husbands aren't to make the wife submit to them, but the wife does so of her own volition by the help of the Holy Spirit.

One of the powerful and practical aspects about this is that the more a wife lives out her role in marriage, God uses it to grow both her and her husband. Redeemed Eve views submission as fighting the temptation of the first Eve who failed to live in light of her high calling given to her by God.

Jesus defines the value of the wife—not the culture.

What makes submission powerful is that the woman is equal to the man in value. She is powerful in how she differs functionally from him. For a gifted (sometimes more gifted) person to willingly submit to a sinner-turned-saint, someone who is in the process of their growth, requires tremendous power. God uses it to grow the husband in being more like Jesus and a more worthy man to follow.

It's about Faith: Faith in God's way is what keeps us safe. Under the proper circumstances is a man and woman who know Jesus as Savior growing in their respective walk with Jesus together and individually walking in their God-ordained roles by faith. Faith is the key to submission. Eve had a belief issue—a stronghold—which made her doubt the character of how God had set up things for their good. When we don't trust God's intentions for our good, we make a mess. Let's hear what a few godly women have to say about this:

- I have discovered that the fundamental issue in relation to submission really comes down to my willingness to trust

God and to place myself under His authority. When I am willing to obey Him, I find it is not nearly so difficult or threatening to submit to the human authorities He has placed in my life.[87]

- Submission without faith is slavery. Submission with faith is power! It takes faith to believe that God is correcting a relationship, situation or circumstance when all outward signs show the opposite. "For we walk by faith, not by sight" (2 Cor. 5:7).[88]

- One common misunderstanding is that submission of a wife to her husband is a burden, a "cross that the wife must bear." However, this is counter to the Bible's true teaching. The submission of a godly wife is more than a duty, it should be her heart's delight.[89]

- What are we liberated from? First, we are free from an "image" or "identity" that suggests we are inferior and subservient. Second, we are released from a prison whose bars represent rebellion, defensiveness, contempt and frustration. That prison's guards are unbelief and its walls are fear. And there is but one key that will unlock the doors: the key of faith.[90]

Submission, when understood as faith in the Lord, hopefully changes everything.

I was on my first pastoral assignment after seminary, and the Lord made it very clear that it was time that we transition from the church where we were serving. I was teaching at a Bible college as an adjunct professor in my twenties, preaching three services, and overseeing several major aspects of the church. At the same time, my wife was extremely sick and pregnant with our second child. I had no prospects, but I sensed that if I didn't move on, it would have been disobedience.

At the time, my wife was on the transplant list, and leaving would have caused us to have to be placed on the transplant list in another region (which would place her at the bottom). She willingly followed me out of that ministry assignment. The Lord ultimately took care of us. We got four calls after we resigned in faith.

The faith she demonstrated by submitting to me, following Jesus, has been used by God to grow me in my willingness to die for her and love even more. When I look back, she made submission look easy. She didn't once call me less than a man, or criticize me. Now maybe in her mind she did that, but all I knew in that situation was a gracious woman of faith trusting that her crazy husband heard from Jesus. Both of us grew in our oneness, and that situation has been a defining moment in our walks with the Lord. We shared together and saw how God used it to shape us both.

Transformative Silence: Before a movie comes on in the theater, all of the noises that are usually prominent during life are not coming from the screen, they are coming from the audience. They aren't being blasted through Dolby Digital surround sound, the sounds of life are echoing between armrests and seat backs. Everything from babies crying, to rattling of paper, chewing popcorn, to slurping the last bit of soda, cell phones, and talking—the sounds of the audience fill the theater. But when the lights go down, and the projector fires up for the previews, something happens to all of the noise. It all stops.

It is an unspoken social contract; audience members will be silent when a movie—one everyone in the theater has paid money to see—has begun showing in public. The purpose of this social phenomenon is to be quiet in the theater while the movie is playing so that no one in the audience is distracted from the main attraction.

One of the ways wives can work against the main attraction of God's work in her husband is not recognizing the power of silence. Now I'm not saying that there aren't needed times for the husband to be respectfully, verbally engaged. But the Bible has much to say about the negative impact the persistent voice of a wife gnawing at the heart of a husband can have. A part of being a gospel woman and a redeemed Eve is to trust the Lord to relegate how you will communicate:

> A wife's quarreling is a continual dripping of rain. (Prov. 19:13b)

> A continual dripping on a rainy day and a quarrelsome wife are alike. (Prov. 27:15)

> It is better to live in a corner of the housetop than in a house shared with a quarrelsome wife. (Prov. 21:9)

> It is better to live in a desert land than with a quarrelsome and fretful woman. (Prov. 21:19)

All of the above "means 'vexation; anger.' The woman is not only characterized by a quarrelsome spirit, but also anger—she is easily vexed (cf. NAB 'vexatious'; NASB 'vexing'; ASV, NRSV 'fretful'). The translation 'easily-provoked' conveys this idea well."[91] This is an accurate portrait of the old Eve. However, the new Eve is in an ever-growing picture of the image of Christ. God transforms her into a woman who "does him good, and not harm, all the days of her life" (Prov. 31:12). Jesus restores women with the ability to move toward this, and God uses that growth as a means of growth for her husband.

Although 1 Peter 3:1 is probably more about an unbelieving husband, it can also apply to a believing husband as well: "Likewise, wives, be subject to your own husbands, so that even if some do not obey the word, they may be won without a word by the conduct of their wives."

"Winning," of course, is in regards to bringing someone into the faith. Yet, from an application standpoint, how many of us believing husbands need to be won practically to the gospel? Winning a husband without a word demonstrates strength, power, and beauty. It demonstrates respect to the husband, even when he doesn't deserve it.

The power of the gospel restrains the female powerhouse who could chop down the tree of the male ego. Being more powerful in Jesus, she restrains her vexation and leaves it in the hands of the Lord. She allows her commitment to the Lord to possess her need to be right.

A godly husband will, at some point, have his eyes opened to the faithfulness of a wife who doesn't bring up everything that she can. Her mouth can sue him for many offenses, but she uses the Spirit's fruit of self-control to bypass her need to be right. She puts on Christ this way: "For this is how the holy women who hoped in God used to adorn themselves, by submitting to their own husbands" (1 Pet. 3:5). After a while, the wife who reflects Jesus by submitting to fallen creation will win him. How my life has been changed by my wife's powerful prayers and submission!

The submissive married woman is a woman of faith, strength, and power! No, that is not a contradiction, but a consistent paradox: "[Women] are liberated by the very principle that Satan has worked so hard to distort: submission."[92]

Conclusion

Marriage is a wonderful entity that God has made. He uses it to display Jesus' relationship with the church. As new Eve and Jesus, the New Adam, they work in concert with one another to display what the first Adam and Eve failed to do. Because of their disobedience (particularly Adam's), sin entered the world and caused man to be separated from God, one another, and the rest of creation. God, through the gospel, reconnects man and woman with one another, individually to Himself, and to all of creation. Jesus' redemption of both aids them in being gracious growth mechanisms for the each other. What a great means of grace husbands and wives are to be for one another when by faith and filled with the Spirit both maximize their God-ordained role. If you want to unleash gospel growth in your family, start by serving your spouse as a godly husband or godly wife.

CHAPTER 9

The Local Church and Spiritual Growth

One of the central ways in which we as believers are grown into the image of Jesus is through the local church. In *Total Church,* Steve Timmis and Tim Chester write, "Church is not another ball for me to juggle but that which defines who I am and gives Christlike shape to my life."[93] In the NT, God uses the church the most by the sheer volume of outlets it provides as the main tool conformity to the image of Christ. You will never fully unleash the transformative, Spirit-empowered power of gospel growth in your life apart from a proper understanding and love of the local church.

Community

Koinonia is the word in the NT for community. It points to the idea of fellowship, partnership, and sharing. Commonality is the idea. Blood-bought believers share the same position in Christ—it is what binds us together. Jesus saves us, and what follows is gathering in practical proximity to one another. The practical, local gathering together of the church is what marks the local church. You don't love the church if you don't gather with a church.

Chester and Timmis say it rightly:

> By becoming a Christian, I belong to God and I belong to my brothers and sisters. It is not that I belong to God and then make a decision to join a local church. My being in Christ means being in Christ with those others who are in Christ.[94]

Biblical community is the interweaving and sharing of the life in Christ with the body of Christ. Biblical community is the context in which the church's connectedness to one another gives birth to transformation. Through both accountability and encouragement, we are conformed into the image of Christ.

The church community is the place in which discipleship happens. In many churches, pastoral leadership is held with the greatest responsibility for discipleship. But if you survey the NT, you will see that discipleship is given over to the entire church community (Heb. 5:11–12). All are called to take the initiative for their brothers and sisters to be conformed to the image of Jesus.

Community and fellowship are more than meals and games; it is where we find belonging, hope, and transformation. Community is messy! It is messy because you have unfinished people intersecting their broken lives with others who are broken as well. We use the tools of the gospel—namely faith, hope, and love—to faithfully walk with one another on the continuum of gospel growth.

THE LOCAL CHURCH AND SPIRITUAL GROWTH

Holy Spirit, Gospel, Faith Community

The local church is the sphere of Holy Spirit activity among God's people. Ephesians 5 makes that clear. When the church community is injured by disobedience that breaks peace, the emulsifier of the community becomes grieved. The grief that the Spirit brings to the body is His way of drawing us back into fellowship with one another (if it is possible). Therefore, the community of the church is a community of the Spirit.

Being a community of the Spirit is more than spiritual gifts, but the presence of a spiritual binder that aids us in pushing past ourselves toward one another. Healthy churches are communities that use the Word and the Spirit to bind it tightly. Failure to use the Word or the Spirit has disastrous consequences.

Although community is formed by faith in the gospel, and is empowered by the Holy Spirit, it is forged by *love*. Love is the fruitful outworking of the Spirit in the life of the community. Hear these words:

A missional people walking in the Spirit, led by the Spirit, and sowing the Spirit manifests the fruit of the Spirit. The very phrase "fruit of the Spirit" emphasizes divine empowerment rather than human works. It is God's life-giving presence, the Holy Spirit, who informs, sustains, and guides communities of "faith working through love" (5:6). Yet believers are not called to passivity by these works. These works require active obedience as believers in community learn to live as God's people together in a fallen world. As both certain evidence that God's redemptive future has dawned and the absolute guarantee of its final consummation, the Spirit empowers this community to manifest love, to work toward peace, to express patience, kindness, and goodness, and to exhibit gentleness and self-control (Gal. 5:22). In this way, the Holy Spirit alone is the antidote to the works of the flesh.[95]

The Spirit, the gospel, and faith move the people of God toward God and toward one another. Love is that which acknowledges that no one has to earn his or her keep. Love is the unconditional, volitional decision to be committed to one another as an expression of God's love for us. All in all, community is a faith fight that we endure together.

Divisiveness

I wish this wasn't the case, but divisiveness is the enemy of the spiritual growth of a church. *Heresy* is a word casually thrown around by evangelical Christians to speak of false doctrine, yet when I look in my Bible, I see something different. Don't get me wrong, false teachers and false doctrine must be condemned, as Peter states in 2 Peter 2. He doesn't mince words when it comes to the work of false teachers.

The word for division in the NT is the word from which we get heresy. Heresy is a *person* not merely a *doctrine*. People who divide the community to the point where an issue becomes the center of the church rather the Lord Jesus Christ are heretics. They are divisive people. Paul tells the Corinthians that anyone who would destroy the church of God, He will destroy them. And Paul speaks about this in the context of the need for the Corinthians to grow spiritually.

With this in mind, divisiveness is a sin that Yahweh calls an abomination in Proverbs 6:19. The Bible states that the Lord *hates* when people sew discord among those who have intimacy with another. The NT goes ever further; it speaks of its effect on those who are not yet rooted in God's Word and the gospel.

> I appeal to you, brothers, to watch out for those who cause divisions and create obstacles contrary to the doctrine that you have been taught; avoid them. For such persons do not serve our Lord Christ, but their own appetites, and by smooth talk and flattery they deceive the hearts of the naive. (Rom. 16:17–18)

Scripture makes it clear that they are enemies of community spiritual growth.

Titus 3:10 tells us to warn them two times, and if they don't repent, they must be promptly removed from the church. People who are divisive seek for the community to be aligned with them rather than the gospel. The opposite of a gospel-centered church is a divided one. We must extend grace to them for the purpose of repentance, but if they continue in this they must be transitioned.

I have dealt with this so many times during the tenure of my ministry. It is always painful. I have seen young believers have their faith hijacked, and people become disillusioned with the local church because of it. Divisiveness never produces gospel fruit, but bitterness and anguish that don't get solved. Because of this, we must engage this issue with great courage.

The One Anothers

The "one anothers" are the means for the church to be a mutual discipleship community. Everyone edifies each other in the context of community. Throughout the New Covenant we see a common theme, the "one anothers." Here is a compiled list with included biblical references:

Unity: One third of the one-another commands deal with the unity of the church.

1. Be at peace with one another (Mark 9:50).
2. Don't grumble among one another (John 6:43).
3. Be of the same mind with one another (Rom. 12:16; 15:5).
4. Accept one another (Rom. 15:7).
5. Wait for one another before beginning the Eucharist (1 Cor. 11:33).
6. Don't bite, devour, and consume one another—seriously, guys, don't eat each other (Gal. 5:15).
7. Don't boastfully challenge or envy one another (Gal. 5:26).
8. Gently, patiently tolerate one another (Eph. 4:2).
9. Be kind, tender-hearted, and forgiving to one another (Eph. 4:32).
10. Bear with and forgive one another (Col. 3:13).
11. Seek good for one another, and don't repay evil for evil (1 Thess. 5:15).
12. Don't complain against one another (James 4:11; 5:9).
13. Confess sins to one another (James 5:16).

Love: One third of them instruct Christians to love one another.

1. Love one another (John 13:34; 15:12, 17; Rom. 13:8; 1 Thess. 3:12; 4:9; 1 Pet. 1:22; 1 John 3:11; 4:7, 11; 2 John 5).
2. Through love, serve one another (Gal. 5:13).
3. Tolerate one another in love (Eph. 4:2).
4. Greet one another with a kiss of love (1 Pet. 5:14).
5. Be devoted to one another in love (Rom. 12:10).

Humility: About 15 percent stress an attitude of humility and deference among believers.

1. Give preference to one another in honor (Rom. 12:10).
2. Regard one another as more important than yourselves (Phil. 2:3).
3. Serve one another (Gal. 5:13).
4. Wash one another's feet (John 13:14).
5. Don't be haughty: be of the same mind (Rom. 12:16).
6. Be subject to one another (Eph. 5:21).
7. Clothe yourselves in humility toward one another (1 Pet. 5:5).

Misc.: Here's the rest:

1. Do not judge one another, and don't put a stumbling block in a brother's way (Rom. 14:13).
2. Greet one another with a kiss (Rom. 16:16; 1 Cor. 16:20; 2 Cor. 13:12).
3. Husbands and wives: don't deprive one another of physical intimacy (1 Cor. 7:5).
4. Bear one another's burdens (Gal. 6:2).

5. Speak truth to one another (Eph. 4:25).

6. Don't lie to one another (Col. 3:9).

7. Comfort one another concerning the resurrection (1 Thess. 4:18).

8. Encourage and build up one another (1 Thess. 5:11).

9. Stimulate one another to love and good deeds (Heb. 10:24).

10. Pray for one another (James 5:16).

11. Be hospitable to one another (1 Pet. 4:9).[96]

All of the "one anothers" work as means for the Lord to bind us in unity, love, and humility. I would add that this is not a perfect division of the list because the verses overlap categories. These provide framework for discipleship and encouragement in the body. These are commands to be pursued persistently. Every Christian in the local church mustn't merely seek these *from* others, but be these *for* others. Too many times in the body, we find ourselves seeking to be on the receiving end of these but not on the giving end of them. We as a community of the Holy Spirit must give *and* receive. The "one anothers" aren't given to a special group of believers, but to all of the body to share in the context of the local church. With this in mind, we may begin to understand how vital the body of Christ is when you just read the list.

Counsel

In earlier years of leading a young church, I felt our spiritual immaturity. It seemed like my shepherding was mainly in the area of counsel. Because of that, pastoring required me to take on the role of a spiritual parent—everything from helping people with basic life decisions, career direction, ministry development, and relationship advice. As others became equipped in their spiritual maturity, we became a community of counselors.

Counsel is a central component of how we discern the will of God. The Bible, the Holy Spirit, counsel in the body, and circumstances (at times) are the means God can use to speak to us. An individual can work through something alone, but we need others to get a bird's-eye view on life. God's Word says, "Plans are established by counsel; by wise guidance wage war" (Prov. 20:18). Counsel helps provide direction as a course of action. We never grow out of needing godly counsel.

Spiritual Gifts

When we teach on spiritual gifts in our local church, I always get questions about the sign gifts and how the body can use them. Rarely do I get people who are concerned about the higher gifts, and how they can serve the body. I'm always asked about tongues and prophecy, never service and helps. It might surprise you, I actually believe it's exegetically reasonable to say that the so-called "sign gifts" haven't ceased, but are still in operation. Just as long as they are used within the framework of biblical parameters, I'm fine (with tons of discernment).

Gifts are a huge part of the body's development. The phrase "build up" is the act of bringing something closer to fullness or completion, as if assisting in the construction of an incomplete building and figuratively, spiritual encouragement making one more able, edifying, or building up.[97] When building up other believers we are supposed to support God's work of sanctification in their lives. Although God is the one that completes the work, we serve them in order that we might participate in His work. What an honor and privilege it is for us to be able to be participants and tools in the hands of God to grow our sisters and brothers in Jesus Christ.

There are people who have the gift of helps and service that I could not imagine our ministry continuing without. Their contribution has served people in ways that communicate care and have been used by God to heal church hurt. But 1 Corinthians 13 tells us that every believer has the gift of love. The gift of love is not a gift a member of the body can fail to bring along with them. In having the gift of love, we must love out of the love that God demonstrated His love in Christ. Every act of building the body up must have love at its core. No gift given to the body works without love.

Shepherds

True Shepherds are a grace given by Jesus to the church to give oversight to their spiritual growth. Pastors bear a major responsibility for the growth for God's people. These roles aren't mere titles, but a calling by God for everyone who qualifies for the office. No matter what role on the team you play—senior pastor, associate pastor, etc.—the responsibility to shepherd must be shared among all the pastors because the Bible says so.

Whether one oversees specific ministry areas for the purpose of organizing the work—youth, outreach worship, or stewardship, etc.—biblically, when you add pastor or elder to the equation, it changes the dynamic of the responsibility.

Our Western context needs for accomplishing the mission of Christ must not be devoid of any of the following categories. Some pastors do these in differing capacities, but on some level, all pastors are responsible for them. These are what I have come to call the categories of shepherding. Jesus perfectly does all of these as the chief Shepherd. Pastors' enablement to help the body grow flows from Him. The categories of shepherding are:

- Lead (1 Tim. 5:17)
- Feed (Ezek. 34)
- Care (Ezek. 34)
- Protect (Titus 1)

Lead: In 1 Timothy 5:17 the word *rule* is used of the role of all elders, but some elders bear more leadership responsibility than others. *Rule* is translated better as "lead" or "direct." While shepherding the flock, the leadership of the elders directs the sheep toward various pastures. Pastors give oversight to the spiritual direction of God's people.

One can say that leadership is the overarching role that permeates the rest of the shepherding categories. In essence, this includes vision, structure, infrastructure, preaching and teaching direction, care, knowing, and protecting. All of these are ways in which a pastor leads. Pastors are commanded to lead the flock.

> Shepherd the flock of God that is among you, exercising oversight, not under compulsion, but willingly, as God would have you; not for shameful gain, but eagerly; not domineering over those in your charge, but being examples to the flock. And when the chief Shepherd appears, you will receive the unfading crown of glory. (1 Pet. 5:2–4)

Jesus, as our Shepherd, leads us beside the still waters. Jesus gave the disciples clarity on what His plans were for them and in general while on earth. Sheep must know where they are going. They must know their shepherd. Timothy Witmer, in *The Shepherd Leader,* says:

> In leading the flock shepherds must be motivated by love for the Lord and for the well-being of the sheep. It must be evident to the congregation that the leadership of the elders is exercised for the good of the people and not for the benefit of the leaders. Even when leaders are developing plans on the macro level, this should take into account their interaction with the sheep on the micro level.[98]

Shepherd-leaders help the church to have a clear direction of the will of God for it. That is why Peter delegated anything that didn't keep them before the face of God and His Word (Acts 6). Even in the Jerusalem council (Acts 15), we see that the letter was sent for the sanctification of the Gentile church. When the body has clear leadership, it aids in building people's confidence in the Lord, His Word, and His church.

Feed: "Especially those who labor in preaching and teaching" (1 Tim. 5:17)—this statement says a lot. Preaching and teaching are central to the shepherding roles of pastors. Feeding happens in different ways.

Mainly, pastors set the doctrinal standard for the entire congregation. They are guardians of the gospel, if you will. As guardians of the gospel, they are to make sure that the historic Christian faith is faithfully passed to the generation of believers. They are responsible for in their local church.

Feeding happens in various settings, but particularly in public worship. In Ezekiel 34 God makes it clear how important feeding His sheep was. It was in many ways central to how He judged how well they were doing. This is why Timothy was exhorted to preach the Word, in and out of season, and not to do so for sordid gain. Faithful shepherds do not preach anything but the Word of God. People need a community of courageous gospel heralds to feed them. In Ezekiel, when the shepherds were not feeding the sheep, they became anemic and sick. Feeding the sheep is what the Spirit uses to grow the flock.

Care: Pastors must build a place for the broken and engage them. Church hurt is rampant and life hurt is even worse. The church is a hospital for the sick. People come to the church for care when they feel stunted in their growth, or when they are going through a hard season in life.

Ezekiel 34:4 says, "The weak you have not strengthened, the sick you have not healed, the injured you have not bound up, the strayed you have not brought back, the lost you have not sought, and with force and harshness you have ruled them." Either by equipping the body for care, or by direct contact, pastors must make sure that people are cared for in the church. When people don't feel legitimately cared for, it impacts how they operate in other areas of the church that might be connecting points for gospel growth. I say legitimately, because sometimes people want the church to be built around their individual needs and neediness, rather than the gospel.

Protect: Earlier we addressed the issue of false teachers/prophets and division in the church. Shepherds need the rod of protection in their hands for the good of the flock. Pastors have to protect the church from itself and from others. Danger comes from the inside and the outside; the church needs to be protected. Several passages communicate this. For example, Titus 1 says, "For there are many who are insubordinate, empty talkers and deceivers, especially those of the circumcision party. They must be silenced, since they are upsetting whole families by teaching for shameful gain what they ought not to teach" (vv. 10–11). Also, 1 Timothy 1, says:

> As I urged you when I was going to Macedonia, remain at Ephesus so that you may charge certain persons not to teach any different doctrine, nor to devote themselves to myths and endless genealogies, which promote speculations rather than the stewardship from God that is by faith. (vv. 3–4)

I remember one of many occasions when my fellow elders and I had to confront several men who were preying on women in the church. In some cases, the women couldn't imagine that they were being preyed on until it was too late. But as a pastor, I am willing to be hated by the sheep in my efforts to pry anyone away from them who would seek to hang a millstone around their neck. If pastors are passive in their protection, sheep can be tossed to and fro by those who prove to be detrimental to their sanctification.

Witmer drops more gospel wisdom on this issue as well:

> Christ's undershepherds are called upon to protect his sheep. The challenge in protecting real sheep is that they are such a helpless lot. They only have teeth on one jaw, so the worst pain they can inflict on an adversary is a good pinch! This is why they need a strong protector. Shepherds need to be aware not only of the vulnerability and weaknesses of the individual sheep but also of the wolves that threaten their well-being.[99]

Paul even challenged the Ephesian church to remove elders who were among them that would seek their own way (Acts 20). In some cases protection looks like disciplining wayward sheep whose sin is causing damage that could be leavening the flock with the yeast of their sin. Allowing some to remain could create a cancerous community. In these cases shepherds must lead the church in disciplining those who would persist in damaging the flock. However, true repentance will lead to true restoration which will grow the soul of the flock as well.

Worship

A worshipper is anyone who has trusted Jesus Christ. It is clear that this identity permeates every area of life, not just our church gatherings. However, we will speak here in regards to the intersection between worship and the local church. Again, some of what we will say will overlap with some aspects of what has been said, but there is enough meat in the Bible for worship to stand on its own.

Gatherings: Hebrews 10:25 makes it clear. Not gathering with God's people in a consistent local church, where one can be known and know others, is neglect. We all need encouragement to continue the race. Gatherings of all kinds with Jesus at the center are needed to be a Holy Spirit encouragement to the faith of all who believe. There has to be different gatherings to know and be known by God's people. You show me anyone who is habitually distant from the church, and I will show you a person who is experiencing very limited growth.

Preaching and Teaching: Earlier we discussed the fact that one of the reasons pastors are placed in the church is to feed it. Now we will talk about the need to seek solid biblical teaching and preaching as a sheep. *Seek* is the operative word here.

In the midst of Paul writing his final letter, he tells his son in the faith, Timothy, that people won't endure sound doctrine. Most times when I read 2 Timothy 4, I focus on those who will fall away. But the text implies that it takes endurance to absorb healthy doctrine. Healthy doctrine can sometimes be that medicine that you have to take, but is either hard to swallow or that which we have a taste aversion to. Getting spiritually healthy through solid teaching and preaching doesn't always feel good. We have to endure by God's power, even when truth can be challenging. Paul tells Timothy, some people are going to get tired of being challenged and hearing about sin and their need to repent. They will want to be told what their entitled flesh wants to hear.

Good healthy preaching and teaching on a regular basis helps to set the tone for our spiritual lives. It sets the tone for disciple-making in the church. Titus, another spiritual son of Paul, is told to teach what accords with sound doctrine (Titus 2:1). His faithful plowing would saturate and transcend genders and generations, causing their hearts to be healthy.

Good, healthy preaching also points regularly to the gospel. It is easy to miss the fact that believers—not just unbelievers—need to be exposed to the gospel. Not necessarily an altar-call gospel presentation, but a rehearsal of the gospel that *both* saves and grows us. The gospel is the hopeful empowerment in expositional preaching. Faith comes by hearing. The more we hear the word of truth in the gospel, our faith is strengthened.

Praise and Worship: One of the "one anothers" is musical exhortation. Gathering with the saints for public worship must have soul-stirring truths that are packed into melodies. In Ephesians 5:19–20 we are told that gatherings of the saints should be a melodic truth exchange. In this we are having our God bandwidth expanded. This Spirit fills us as we soak in the truths of God into our heart. God Himself dwells inside of us, as the Word says, "Yet you are holy, enthroned on the praises of Israel" (Ps. 22:3). "The metaphorical language pictures the LORD as sitting enthroned as king in his temple, receiving the praises that his people Israel offer up to him."[100] I know they didn't have it better under the Law. The presence of Christ through Spirit fills our gatherings as we are edified by His filling and controlling presence. Worship gatherings are therapeutic to the weary soul.

Giving: Abused as it has been, it is an area that needs to be unapologetically pursued for the building up of God's people. For a while, many church planters I know (including myself) almost found ourselves apologizing for asking for resources necessary to serve God.

I can vividly remember one Sunday when I was done with it. I got up and told the church, "We are sorry for your past church hurt, but we are no longer building our appeal for worshipping the Lord through giving around your broken past." I began to quote the bold requests of Paul throughout the NT. In addition, I told the church that Philippians was mainly a financial support letter to the church. My elders and I stated our commitment to help people walk through their hurt, but it had been enough time for our appeals to be received. Two to three years later, this inner-city church became self-supported.

Jesus and Paul let God's people know that giving is deeply connected to the heart. Jesus states, "For where your treasure is, there your heart will be also" (Matt. 6:21). Although this verse is more than money, it points to everything we treasure. Let me be clear,

I'm not just talking about the Sunday offering (as important as that is), but I am speaking of merciful, sacrificial giving. Believers see a need in the body and commit to aid. I remember while in seminary, we went through one of many hard financial times. While at Oak Cliff Bible Fellowship we built deep community life in that church. Many a day were we fed by Christians in hard times. Two families in particular knew my wife and I had no family in Dallas, Texas. They made it their point to make sure we were at the table eating and carrying food home. Now as a church planter, we do the same for others. Their generosity was a tool of growth for us.

Baptism: Obedience to the mission of Christ includes, not only making disciples, but baptizing them as well. Jesus, before He returned to the right hand of the Father, said to His disciples, "Go therefore and make disciples of all nations, baptizing them in the name of the Father and of the Son and of the Holy Spirit" (Matt. 28:19). An essential part of gospel growth in a local church is following Christ's command to baptize and be baptized. More than that, we ought to—if we are truly desiring to be conformed into the image of Christ—follow His example in His own baptism (Matt. 3:16).

Communion: What in the world does communion have to do with being conformed to the image of Jesus? It is that which causes us to reflect deeply on what was done for us and take it in a manner that by faith nurtures us in deep gospel reflection. First Corinthians 11 calls us to take it in a worthy manner. A better question is: How do we take something in a worthy manner when we aren't worthy in the first place?

"Paul's logic is this: The Lord's Supper proclaims the Lord's death. Those whose behavior at the Lord's Supper does not conform to what that death entails effectively shift sides. They leave the Lord's side and align themselves with the rulers of this present age who crucified the Lord (1 Cor. 2:8; cf. Heb. 6:5). This explains how they make themselves so vulnerable to God's judgment."[101] The Lord's Table is for those who know that they are in desperate need of God and how their lives are nothing without His sacrificial work. To take it in an unworthy manner is to think that you are worthy of anything apart from Him.

Conclusion

What a great place to end this chapter on: our desperate need for Jesus. We need the church as God's tool of conformity to the image of Christ. As all of the means mentioned in this book, the church isn't supposed to be a leash, but a mechanism for the body to be *Unleashed: Being Conformed to the Image of Christ.* May we pursue building healthy churches by the power of the Spirit and by faith in the glorious gospel.

CHAPTER 10

Conclusion: When It's All Said and Done

Some bright morning when this life is over
I'll fly away
To that home on God's celestial shore
I'll fly away
I'll fly away oh glory
I'll fly away (in the morning)
When I die hallelujah by and by
I'll fly away
When the shadows of this life have gone
I'll fly away
Like a bird from these prison walls I'll fly
I'll fly away

J esus' second coming could be any day. Our process of spiritual growth will be brought to its full completion, and we will be fully saved. We have been justified by faith in Jesus, we are being sanctified by faith in Jesus, and we will be glorified by faith in Jesus.

The doctrine of glorification is the consummation of all things through Jesus practically placing all things under His feet. It is sanctification when it is fully complete.

Although Jesus is the King of kings, the distribution of authority seen and unseen is deeply fallen. From fallen governments and spiritual rulers, His kingdom is in the state of the "already, but not yet."

"Already," in that He is King and sitting enthroned at the right hand of the Father. "Not yet," in that His rule isn't fully realized by His rebellious creation and we feel the effects of the Fall now. However, His kingdom will come, and when it does, all will know. All will know and see Him in all of His glory (Rev. 20).

The Hope of Glory

The blessed hope of Jesus' imminent return motivates our growth *now*. Paul speaks of the two advents of Jesus in Titus 2:11–13:

> For the grace of God has appeared, bringing salvation for all people, training us to renounce ungodliness and worldly passions, and to live self-controlled, upright, and godly lives in the present age, waiting for our blessed hope, the appearing of the glory of our great God and Savior Jesus Christ.

The first advent was His incarnation. The second advent will be His full—not partial—return when He ends the era of response to Him by faith and begins to usher in the eternal state. We are more than equipped by God for what is necessary to look like Him, *now*. All of the tools of growth presented in this book must be sought after by faith in Jesus. When we do so, God the Spirit uses them to grow us immensely in Jesus Christ. As we connect and engage every area by faith, we will find ourselves growing in varying measures into the image of Jesus.

When Jesus returns, He will:

1. Glorify living and sleeping saints (1 Thess. 4; Rev. 20)
2. Eternally punish all the sentient enemies of God (Rev. 19–20)
3. Judge the fallen nations (Rev. 19)
4. Destroy death and hades (Rev. 20)
5. Eternally punish all unbelieving humans (Rev. 20)
6. Re-create a groaning universe (Rev. 21)
7. Hand the universal Kingdom Crown to God the Father (1 Cor. 15; Rev. 21)
8. The Father Calls for the universal bowing of all to Jesus (Phil. 2)

And for all of this, the saint has a front-row seat too.

Until then, let's live for Him by faith in the glorious gospel.

Unleash the power of the Spirit to wreck your idols and replace them with the Second Adam on the altar of your heart.

Be conformed to the image of Christ.

Amen.

NOTES

1. See http://www.thegospelcoalition.org/article/martin-luther-on -marriage-as-a-school-of-character.

2. Timothy Keller, *The Centrality of the Gospel,* The Movement Newsletter, Redeemer Presbyterian Church.

3. Andrew M. Davis, *An Infinite Journey: Growing toward Christlikeness* (Greenville, SC: Ambassador International, 2014). Kindle edition, locations 478–81.

4. David Peterson, *Possessed by God: A New Testament Theology of Sanctification and Holiness* in New Studies in Biblical Theology Series, ed. D. A. Carson (Downers Grove, IL: InterVarsity Press, 1995), Kindle edition, locations 154–56.

5. J. V. Fesko, *A Christian's Pocket Guide to Growing in Holiness* (Scotland, UK: Christian Focus Publications, 2012), Kindle edition, locations 134–36.

6. Peterson, *Possessed by God,* Kindle locations 496–502.

7. As G. F. Hawthorne, 98, and others suggest.

8. J. Warren, "Work Out," 128, rightly observes that the rendering "work *out*" draws attention to "thoroughness" rather than "exteriority."

9. F. F. Bruce, 56.

10. W. Hendriksen, 120.

11. Peter T. O'Brien, *The Epistle to the Philippians: A Commentary on the Greek Text* (Grand Rapids, MI: Eerdmans, 1991), 279.

12. Peterson, *Possessed by God,* Kindle locations 1490–98.

13. Arthur W. Pink, *The Holy Spirit* (Blacksburg, VA: Wilder Publications, 2008), 7.

14. Ibid.

15. Cf. Gen. 1:2; Exod. 23:3; 31:3; Num. 11:17–29; Judg. 3:10; 6:34; 2 Kings 2:9, 15–16; Ezek. 2:2; 3:12; 11:1, 5.

16. John 16, note 32 in *The NET Bible* (Biblical Studies Press, 2006). AB—Anchor Bible (a commentary series).

17. Also see Acts 4:8, 31; 9:17; 13:9 (cf. Acts 10, 16, 19).

18. Ephesians 5:18, note 26 in *The NET Bible.*

19. Lincoln, 344. D. B. Wallace, *Greek Grammar,* 375, on the grounds that Christ is the agent of the filling in 4:10, claims that in 5:18: "Believers are to be filled *by* Christ *by means of* the Spirit *with* the content of the fullness of God."

20. Peter T. O'Brien, *The Letter to the Ephesians* (Grand Rapids, MI: Eerdmans Publishing Co., 1999), 391.

21. Sinclair Ferguson, *The Holy Spirit* (Downers Grove, IL: InterVarsity Press, 1995), 89.

22. When we speak of God's communicable attributes, we are referring primarily to His moral attributes such as love, goodness, and kindness. In one sense, we must not forget that there is a basic incommunicability of even these attributes, for insofar as such things as the love and goodness of God are infinite, we cannot imitate them. Nevertheless, because we bear God's image, there is a manner in which we exhibit these attributes by way of analogy. For example, the kind of love we have as creatures is not identical to the kind of love our Creator possesses. However, at the same time, our love is not wholly dissimilar, such that there is no point of contact whatsoever with the love of God. Our Creator loves truly that which is lovely. As regenerate people, we possess the capacity to do the same.

Consider also God's attribute of holiness. The holiness of God encompasses several concepts, including the fact that He is inherently set apart from creation and that He is morally pure, without any hint of darkness or sin. We cannot possess holiness in the sense of being inherently set apart from creation; however, by the renewing work of God's Spirit, Christians are continually purified over the course of our lives (1 John 3:3). See http://www.ligonier.org/learn/devotionals /gods-communicable-attributes.

23. See www.thefreedictionary.com.

24. L. O. Garrett, "Repentance" in D. N. Freedman, A. C. Myers and A. B. Beck (Eds.), *Eerdmans Dictionary of the Bible* (Grand Rapids, MI: Eerdmans, 2000), 1118.

25. See www.Christalone.com/quote/170-Charles-Spurgeon?start=29.

26. Proverbs 28:13, note 37 in *The NET Bible*.

27. Thomas Watson, *Doctrine of Repentance* (Puritan Paperbacks, 1988), 15.

28. Thomas L. Constable, *Notes on 2 Samuel* (Dallas Theological Seminary, 2000 ed.).

29. Proverbs 28:13, note 38 in *The NET Bible*.

30. Ibid., note 39.

31. John Calvin and John Owen, *Commentary on the Epistle of Paul the Apostle to the Hebrews* (Bellingham, WA: Logos Bible Software, 2010), 262.

32. Galatians 3:1, note 2 in *The NET Bible*.

33. Douglas J. Moo, *The Epistle to the Romans* (Grand Rapids, MI: Eerdmans Publishing Co., 1996), 863.

34. Donald S. Whitney, *Spiritual Disciplines for the Christian Life* (Colorado Springs, CO: NavPress, 2014), 48.

35. Fesko, *A Christian's Pocket Guide to Growing in Holiness*, Kindle edition, locations 368–70.

36. John 17:17, note 52 in *The NET Bible*.

37. William Arndt, Frederick W. Danker, and Walter Bauer, *A Greek-English Lexicon of the New Testament and Other Early Christian Literature,* 3rd ed. (Chicago: University of Chicago Press, 2000), 326.

38. Eric Mason, *Manhood Restored: How the Gospel Makes Men Whole* (Nashville: B&H Publishing Group, 2013), 79.

39. See http://www.spurgeon.org/treasury/ps001.htm.

40. Jonathan Edwards, *A Treatise Concerning Religious Affections* (Oak Harbor, WA: Logos Research Systems, Inc., 1996).

41. Whitney, *Spiritual Disciplines for the Christian Life*, 46–47.

42. James Swanson, *Dictionary of Biblical Languages with Semantic Domains: Hebrew (Old Testament),* electronic ed. (Oak Harbor: Logos Research Systems, Inc., 1997).

43. Leonard Ravenhill, *Why Revival Tarries* (Grand Rapids, MI: Baker Publishing Group, 2004), Kindle edition, locations 233–35.

44. Fesko, *A Christian's Pocket Guide to Growing in Holiness,* Kindle edition, locations 469–73.

45. C. E. Arnold, *Zondervan Illustrated Bible Backgrounds Commentary: Hebrews to Revelation,* vol. 4 (Grand Rapids, MI: Zondervan, 2002), 31.

46. Peter T. O'Brien, *The Letter to the Hebrews* (Grand Rapids, MI; Nottingham, England: Eerdmans Pub. Co., 2010), 201.

47. Charles H. Spurgeon, *Lectures to My Students* (Fig Classic Series, 2012), Kindle edition, locations 855–63.

48. Leonard Ravenhill, *Why Revival Tarries* (Grand Rapids, MI: Baker Publishing Group, 2004), 25.

49. Charles A. Wanamaker, *The Epistles to the Thessalonians: A Commentary on the Greek Text* (Grand Rapids, MI: Eerdmans, 1990), 233.

50. Swanson, *Dictionary of Biblical Languages with Semantic Domains: Hebrew (Old Testament),* electronic ed., HGK8143.

51. Jonathan Edwards, *Life and Diary of David Brainerd* (New York: Cosimo, Inc., 2007), 345–46.

52. Gene L. Green, *The Letters to the Thessalonians, The Pillar New Testament Commentary* (Grand Rapids, MI; Leicester, England: W. B. Eerdmans Pub.; Apollos, 2002), 297.

53. Timothy Friberg, Barbara Friberg, and Neva F. Miller, *Analytical Lexicon of the Greek New Testament,* vol. 4 (Grand Rapids, MI: Baker Books, 2000), 392.

54. Paul Lee Tan, *Encyclopedia of 7700 Illustrations: Signs of the Times* (Garland, TX: Bible Communications, Inc., 1996), 1178.

55. Leon Morris, *The Epistle to the Romans* (Grand Rapids, MI; Leicester, England: Eerdmans; InterVarsity Press, 1988), 221.

56. Ibid.

57. Grant R. Osborne, *Romans* (Downers Grove, IL: InterVarsity Press, 2004), 130.

58. Andy Stanley, *Next Generation Leader* (Colorado Springs: Multnomah, 2003), Kindle edition.

59. Friberg, Friberg, and Miller, *Analytical Lexicon of the Greek New Testament,* vol. 4, 290.

60. See http://davidwilkersontoday.blogspot.com/2009/07/dealing-with -our-strongholds.html.

61. See http://www.jamesmacdonald.com/recently-preached/destroying -the-strongholds-in-my-disposition.

62. See Oneplace.com.

63. Tony Evans, *Victory in Spiritual Warfare: Outfitting Yourself for the Battle* (Eugene, OR: Harvest House Publishers, 2011), 169.

64. See http://www.pastoremase.com/good-grief.

65. *Theophany* is God appearing in a physical form of some sort usually to His people to reveal Himself in some definitive way. It is through this means in which God displays mercy, by in some way not allowing His dwelling presence to be experienced in order that His people or others wouldn't be destroyed.

66. Sometimes ancient Near Easterners would also use threshing sledges, which consisted of boards with embedded flint or basalt studs and were drawn over the stalks of grain by donkeys or oxen. See King and Stager, *Life in Biblical Israel,* 89–90.

67. Swanson, *Dictionary of Biblical Languages with Semantic Domains: Hebrew (Old Testament),* electronic ed.

68. J. N. Oswalt, 310, in R. Laird Harris, Gleason L. Archer Jr., and Bruce K. Waltke (eds.), *Theological Wordbook of the Old Testament,* electronic ed. (Chicago: Moody Press, 1999), 148.

69. John H. Walton, *Zondervan Illustrated Bible Backgrounds Commentary (Old Testament) Volume 2: Joshua, Judges, Ruth, 1 & 2 Samuel* (Grand Rapids, MI: Zondervan, 2009), 153–54.

70. Ibid.

71. Roland H. Bainton, *Here I Stand: A Life of Martin Luther* (Nashville: Abingdon Press, 1978), Kindle edition, locations 4036–38.

72. See http://shop.familylife.com/p-1727-marriage-oneness.aspx.

73. Genesis 2:24, note 74 in *The NET Bible.*

74. Ibid., note 72.

75. Ibid., note 73.

76. Genesis 2:25, notes 74–75 in *The NET Bible*.

77. Tony Evans, *The Kingdom Agenda* (Chicago: Moody Publishers, 2013), 221.

78. Genesis 3:16 in *The NET Bible*.

79. Ibid.

80. Timothy Keller, *The Meaning of Marriage: Facing the Complexities of Commitment with the Wisdom of God* (New York: Penguin Group, 2011), 115.

81. Stuart Scott, *The Exemplary Husband: A Biblical Perspective* (Focus Publishing, 2002), Kindle edition, locations 1370–71.

82. Friberg, Friberg, and Miller, *Analytical Lexicon of the Greek New Testament,* vol. 4, 312.

83. Ibid., 194.

84. Stu Weber, *Tender Warrior: Every Man's Purpose, Every Woman's Dream, Every Child's Hope* (The Doubleday Religious Publishing Group, 2006), Kindle edition, locations 1857–64.

85. P. B. Wilson, *Liberated Through Submission* (Harvest House Publishers, 1990), Kindle edition, locations 126–28.

86. O'Brien, *The Letter to the Ephesians*, 416.

87. Nancy Leigh DeMoss, *Lies Women Believe: And the Truth that Sets Them Free* (Chicago: Moody Publishers, 2001), 149.

88. Wilson, *Liberated Through Submission*, Kindle locations 440–42.

89. Martha Peace, *The Excellent Wife: A Biblical Perspective* (Focus Publishing, 1999), Kindle edition, locations 1872–74.

90. Wilson, *Liberated Through Submission*, Kindle locations 1180–83.

91. Proverbs 21:19, note 63 in *The NET Bible*. NAB—The New American Bible, NASB—New American Standard Bible, ASV—American Standard Version (1901), NRSV—New Revised Standard Version (1989).

92. Wilson, *Liberated Through Submission*, Kindle locations 1178–80.

93. Tim Chester and Steve Timmis, *Total Church: A Radical Reshaping around Gospel and Community* (Wheaton, IL: Crossway, 2008), Kindle edition, locations 563–64.

94. Ibid., Kindle locations 507–508.

95. Lois Barrett, *Missional Church: A Vision for the Sending of the Church in North America* (The Gospel and Our Culture Series) (Eerdmans Publishing Co., 1998), Kindle edition, locations 2674–75.

96. Posted on March 9, 2014 by Jeffrey Kranz. See http://overview Bible.com/one-another-infographic. All of these "one anothers" listed here come from this site.

97. Friberg, Friberg, and Miller, *Analytical Lexicon of the Greek New Testament,* vol. 4, 278.

98. Timothy Z. Witmer, *The Shepherd Leader: Achieving Effective Shepherding in Your Church* (Philipsburg, NJ: P&R Publishing, 2010), 156.

99. Ibid., 170.

100. Psalm 22:3, note 6 in *The NET Bible.*

101. David E. Garland, *1 Corinthians, Baker Exegetical Commentary on the New Testament* (Grand Rapids, MI: Baker Academic, 2003), 550.

AVAILABLE SPRING 2016

BEING CONFORMED TO THE IMAGE OF CHRIST

UNLEASHED
BIBLE STUDY

ERIC MASON

Share the *Unleashed Bible Study* in your small group and help others learn what it means to unleash God's power in their lives.